Grade 3

Addison-Wesley Mathematics

Challenges Workbook

▲▼Addison-Wesley Publishing Company

Menlo Park, California ▪ *Reading, Massachusetts* ▪ *New York*
Don Mills, Ontario ▪ *Wokingham, England* ▪ *Amsterdam* ▪ *Bonn*
Sydney ▪ *Singapore* ▪ *Tokyo* ▪ *Madrid* ▪ *San Juan*

Copyright © by Addison-Wesley Publishing Company, Inc.
The workbook pages in this publication are designed to be used with
appropriate duplicating equipment to reproduce copies for classroom
use. Addison-Wesley Publishing Company grants permission to
classroom teachers to reproduce these pages. Printed in the United
States of America. Published simultaneously in Canada.

ISBN 0-201-27311-X

2 3 4 5 6 7 8 9 10 - HC - 95 94 93 92 91

Table of Contents

Add or Subtract?

For each action shown, write a story problem. Ask a classmate to work with you. Have your partner decide what operation to use to solve each problem and write the correct number sentence for the action.

1. Put together _____

_____

_____

_____Add_____ _____ _____ = _____

2. Compare _____

_____

_____

_____ _____ _____ = _____

3. Take away _____

_____

_____

_____ _____ _____ = _____

4. Put together _____

_____

_____

_____ _____ _____ = _____

Addison-Wesley | All Rights Reserved

Let's Go Fishing

Fish the missing numbers out of the pond.

1. $7 - \boxed{} = 5$ **2.** $6 + \boxed{} = 8$ **3.** $8 + \boxed{} = 9$

4. $7 - \boxed{} = 4$ **5.** $8 + \boxed{} = 10$ **6.** $9 - \boxed{} = 7$

7. $8 + \boxed{} = 8$ **8.** $7 + \boxed{} = 10$ **9.** $8 - \boxed{} = 5$

10. $11 + \boxed{} = 14$ **11.** $6 - \boxed{} = 3$ **12.** $8 + \boxed{} = 11$

13. $5 - \boxed{} = 5$ **14.** $8 - \boxed{} = 6$ **15.** $9 + \boxed{} = 10$

16. $10 + \boxed{} = 13$ **17.** $9 - \boxed{} = 6$ **18.** $7 + \boxed{} = 7$

19. $7 - \boxed{} = 7$ **20.** $11 + \boxed{} = 13$ **21.** $12 + \boxed{} = 15$

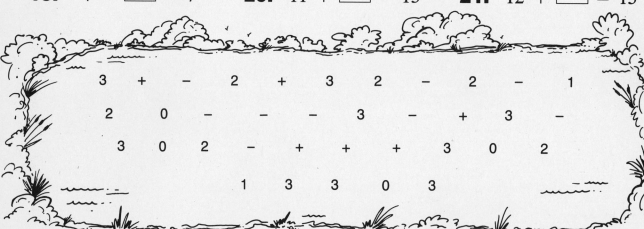

Inside the pond:

3 + − 2 + 3 2 − 2 − 1

2 0 − − − 3 − + 3 −

3 0 2 − + + + 3 0 2

1 3 3 0 3

Fish the missing signs out of the pond.

22. $8 \bigcirc 3 = 5$ **23.** $8 \bigcirc 1 = 7$ **24.** $9 \bigcirc 2 = 7$

25. $9 \bigcirc 2 = 11$ **26.** $9 \bigcirc 3 = 6$ **27.** $11 \bigcirc 2 = 9$

28. $8 \bigcirc 4 = 4$ **29.** $5 \bigcirc 3 = 2$ **30.** $5 \bigcirc 2 = 7$

31. $12 \bigcirc 2 = 14$ **32.** $12 \bigcirc 2 = 10$ **33.** $12 \bigcirc 3 = 15$

34. $14 \bigcirc 3 = 11$ **35.** $9 \bigcirc 1 = 10$ **36.** $11 \bigcirc 2 = 13$

Addison-Wesley | All Rights Reserved

Hidden Facts

There are 36 numbers in the puzzle below. Look across
or down to find as many addition facts as you can.
Put the plus (+) and equal (=) signs where they
belong. Then circle each fact.

3	+ 3	= 6	5	5	10
+					
4	2	1	4	3	8
=					
7	8	16	9	2	7
7	6	6	12	4	15
14	2	8	1	4	5
9	9	18	9	8	17

Addison-Wesley | All Rights Reserved

Magic Squares

Find the sums by completing the number sentences below.

(Make 10.)	(Add the extra ones.)	(Sum)

1. $7 + 6$ $\boxed{7 + 3}$ $+$ ___3___ $=$ ___13___

2. $9 + 3$ $\boxed{}$ $+$ _____ $=$ _____

3. $8 + 4$ $\boxed{}$ $+$ _____ $=$ _____

Complete each box. The sum of the first two numbers in each row must be 10. The sum of all three numbers in each row is given.

4.

8	2	5	→ 15
9			→ 17
	3		→ 11

5.

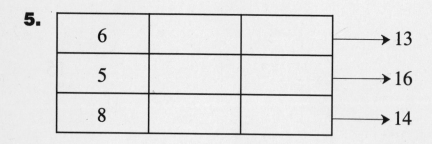

6			→ 13
5			→ 16
8			→ 14

6.

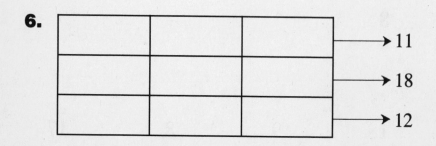

			→ 11
			→ 18
			→ 12

Addison-Wesley | All Rights Reserved

Name _____

Strategy Game

Dear Family,
    This game is designed to challenge and develop your child's thinking skills.
You may wish to play many times as you develop winning strategies.

Rules:
1. There are 2 teams. Each team begins with 14 markers. (To make markers, cut out circles of colored paper. Each team chooses a different color.)
2. On a team's turn, 1 player must cover either 1 or 2 playing squares on the game board below. The 2 teams take turns covering the board.
3. Continue until one team makes the other team cover a fourth square in a row: across, down, or diagonally. The team that covers the fourth square in a row loses.

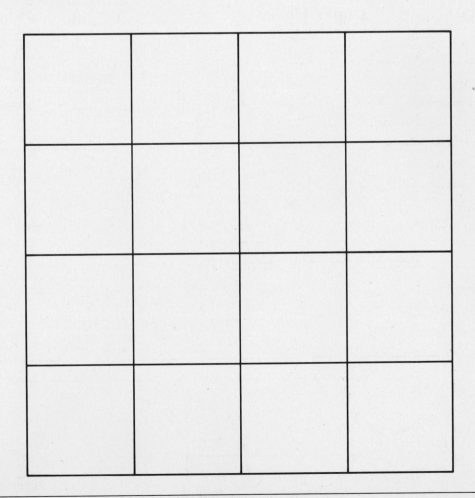

Addison-Wesley | All Rights Reserved

Name _____

What Is the Difference?

> Dear Family,
>   Your child has been learning strategies for finding differences. Help your child complete these exercises.

For each exercise below, decide which strategy you can use to subtract. Then complete one of the boxes.

If you **count up** to find the difference, write the numbers you say on the lines. Then write the answer in the △ .

If you **subtract from 10 and add the extra**, fill in the number sentences. Write the answer in the ☐ .

	Count Up	**Subtract from 10 and add the extra**
1. $\begin{array}{r} 14 \\ -\ 8 \\ \hline \end{array}$	8, ____, ____, ____, ____, ____, ____ △	10 − ____ = ____ ____ + ____ = ☐
2. $\begin{array}{r} 12 \\ -\ 8 \\ \hline \end{array}$	8, ____, ____, ____, ____ △	10 − ____ = ____ ____ + ____ = ☐
3. $\begin{array}{r} 12 \\ -\ 9 \\ \hline \end{array}$	9, ____, ____, ____ △	10 − ____ = ____ ____ + ____ = ☐
4. $\begin{array}{r} 11 \\ -\ 9 \\ \hline \end{array}$	9, ____, ____ △	10 − ____ = ____ ____ + ____ = ☐

Addison-Wesley | All Rights Reserved

Addison-Wesley | All Rights Reserved

Name _____

Bottom of the Bay

Bev and Roger are scuba divers.
They made a map of the bottom of
the bay where they dive. The map
shows the number of minutes
it takes to swim from
one place to another.

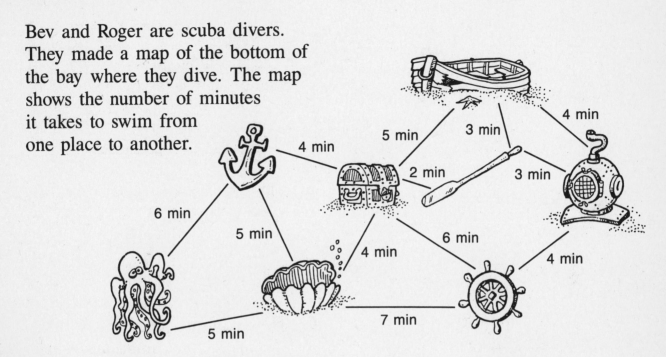

Use a calculator to find how long it takes to swim these paths.

1.

15 min

2.
_____

3.
_____

4.
_____

5.
_____

6.
_____

7. Ring the path that is shorter.

Name _____

Roller Coaster Rides

Read the story. Decide what operation to use to answer each question that can be answered. Write the answers to the questions that **can** be answered. Put an **X** after the questions that **cannot** be answered.

> Nan took 5 roller coaster rides in the morning. She took 7 roller coaster rides in the afternoon. Ted took 9 roller coaster rides in all.

1. How many roller coaster rides did Nan take in all?

_____

2. How many more rides did Nan take in the afternoon than in the morning?

_____

3. How many more rides did Ted take in the afternoon than in the morning?

_____

4. How many more rides did Ted take in the morning than Nan?

_____

5. How many rides did the children take in all?

_____

6. How many rides did Nan and Ted take in the afternoon?

7. How many more rides did Nan take than Ted?

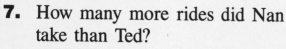

_____

Addison-Wesley | All Rights Reserved

Secret Numbers

Secret Agent 758 thinks the numbers 7, 5, and 8 are her lucky numbers. Write the six different numbers she can make by changing the place values of 7, 5, and 8.

_____ _____

_____ _____

_____ _____

Use the clues below to find out how she uses each of the numbers.

1.
▶ The largest digit is in the tens place.
▶ The smallest digit is in the hundreds place.

Her secret license plate number is _____ .

2.
▶ The digit in the hundreds place is smaller than the digit in the tens place.
▶ The ones digit is the smallest.

Her secret apartment number is _____ .

3.
▶ The sum of the first two digits is 13.
▶ The sum of the last two digits is 12.

Her secret house number is _____ .

4.
▶ The sum of the last two digits is 12
▶ The ones digit is the smallest.

Her secret bank account number is _____ .

5.
▶ The sum of the last two digits is 15.
▶ The 7 is not in the ones place.

Her secret mailbox number is _____ .

Addison-Wesley | All Rights Reserved

Maze Race

Dear Family,
   Our class has just studied reading and writing numbers and putting numbers in order. The game below gives your child an opportunity to share these skills with you.

Ask someone in your family to play a counting game with you. First, cut the page apart so you each have a square. You will each need a crayon to play. Color a path from the start to the end by counting backward. You can move up, down, left, or right. The first one to finish wins.

Start

99	98	95	88	85	84	83	82	81	82
89	97	89	87	86	87	85	75	80	79
95	96	94	88	84	72	73	74	67	78
94	88	90	89	72	71	76	75	76	77
93	92	91	92	69	70	49	50	47	78
94	93	68	67	68	49	48	47	46	45
65	64	65	66	51	50	49	50	47	44
62	63	66	57	58	57	50	51	42	43
61	56	57	56	55	56	51	52	41	44
60	59	58	59	54	53	52	53	40	39

End

Start

99	98	95	88	85	84	83	82	81	82
89	97	89	87	86	87	85	75	80	79
95	96	94	88	84	72	73	74	67	78
94	88	90	89	72	71	76	75	76	77
93	92	91	92	69	70	49	50	47	78
94	93	68	67	68	49	48	47	46	45
65	64	65	66	51	50	49	50	47	44
62	63	66	57	58	57	50	51	42	43
61	56	57	56	55	56	51	52	41	44
60	59	58	59	54	53	52	53	40	39

End

Addison-Wesley | All Rights Reserved

Addison-Wesley | All Rights Reserved

Name _____

Pattern Partners

Imagine that you work with three people in a warehouse. Your job is to ship the correct number of items to stores. The chart below shows the number of each item that is shipped to each store. But some numbers are missing. Work with your team. First identify the four counting patterns used in the chart. Then each team member should choose one pattern and complete part of the chart. Check one another's work to be sure you are filling the orders correctly.

Item	Store 1	Store 2	Store 3	Store 4	Store 5	Store 6
greeting cards	103	203	303	403		
key chains	20	22		26		30
ribbon	35		45	50	55	
postcards	48	58	68		88	
stickers		92	94		98	100
balloons	12		212	312		512
wrapping paper	27	37			67	77
pens		210	215	220		230

Name _____

Picture This

Draw a picture to help you solve each problem.

Example: Terry lives closer to the park than Mark. Cara lives in between Terry and Mark. Amy lives closer to the park than Terry. In what order do the friends live from the park?

Park   A   T   C   M
_____

Answer: __Amy, Terry, Cara, Mark__

1. Four students were in a spelling bee. Frank finished ahead of Beth. Morgan finished after Beth. Elena finished between Beth and Morgan. In what order did the students finish the spelling bee?

_____

Answer: _____

_____

2. Four teams played in the softball play-off. The Turkeys and the Camels beat the Goats. The Camels came in after the Turkeys. The Elephants beat the Turkeys. In what order did the teams finish?

_____

Answer: _____

_____

3. The police station is closer to City Hall than the doctor's office. The market is between the police station and the doctor's office. The library is between the police station and the market. What is the order of buildings from City Hall?

_____

Answer: _____

_____

Use with text pages 38–39.

Addison-Wesley | All Rights Reserved

More and Less

Change the order of these cards to make numbers that fit
each box. Some boxes will have more numbers than others.
Some numbers will fit in more than one box.

1	5	6

1.
More than 225 and
and less than 575

_____

_____

2.
More than 160 and
less than 600

_____

_____

3.
Less than 650 and
more than 550

_____

_____

8	4	3

4.
More than 350 and
less than 800

_____

_____

5.
Less than 425 and
more than 350

_____

_____

6.
More than 450 and
less than 845

_____

_____

7	2	9

7.
More than 690 and
less than 900

_____

_____

8.
More than 290 and
less than 775

_____

_____

9.
More than 750 and
less than 995

_____

_____

Addison-Wesley | All Rights Reserved

February Fun

Study the calendar. Then write a paragraph to describe each event that will take place in February. In your sentences, use ordinal numbers for each calendar date.

FEBRUARY

Sunday	Monday	Tuesday	Wednesday	Thursday	Friday	Saturday
					1 3rd-Grade Play	2
3	4	5	6 Field Trip	7	8	9
10	11 Book Reports Due	12	13	14 Valentine's Day	15	16
17	18 Presidents' Day	19	20	21	22	23 School Art Show
24	25	26	27 Science Fair	28		

_____

_____

_____

_____

Addison-Wesley | All Rights Reserved

Name _____

Mystery Numbers

Analyze the clues to find
these mystery numbers.

1.
When I am rounded to the
nearest ten, I am 60. The
digit in my ones place is 2
more than the digit in my
tens place.

Who am I?

_____

2.
When I am rounded to the
nearest ten, I am 50. The
sum of my digits is 13.

Who am I?

_____

3.
When I am rounded to the
nearest ten, I am 80. The
digit in my tens place is 5
more than the digit in my
ones place.

Who am I?

_____

4.
When I am rounded to the
nearest ten, I am 70. The
difference between my digits
is 3. I can be two different
numbers.

Who am I?

_____

5.
When I am rounded to the
nearest ten, I am 20. But I
am just as close to 10.

Who am I?

_____

6.
When I am rounded to the
nearest ten, I am 40. The
sum of my digits is 8. I can
be two different numbers.

Who am I?

_____ _____

Addison-Wesley | All Rights Reserved

Finding Prices

The school is having a plant sale.
You know about how much each plant is worth.
Use the three numbers to fill in the price tag.

1. 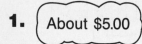 Use 9, 4, and 2.   **2.** 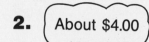 Use 9, 4, and 2.

$ ___ . ___ ___ $ ___ . ___ ___

3.  Use 1, 3, and 5.   **4.**  Use 1, 3, and 5.

$ ___ . ___ ___ $ ___ . ___ ___

5. 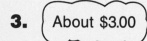 Use 5, 4, and 7.   **6.** 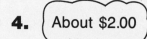 Use 5, 4, and 7.

$ ___ . ___ ___ $ ___ . ___ ___

7.  Use 4, 6, and 9.   **8.** 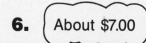 Use 4, 6, and 9.

$ ___ . ___ ___ $ ___ . ___ ___

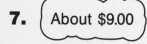

Addison-Wesley | All Rights Reserved

The price tags read: About $5.00, About $4.00, About $3.00, About $2.00, About $8.00, About $7.00, About $9.00, About $6.00.

Math Meet

The Adds and the Subs are two math teams. The teams are writing cheers for the next math meet. Each cheer begins with a question.

Help the teams sort out the questions. Write the questions for addition problems in the Adds' column. Write the questions for subtraction problems in the Subs' column. Now work with a friend to make up a cheer for one team. Write your cheer on a piece of paper. Share your cheer with classmates.

- What is the total?
- What is the difference?
- What is the sum?
- How many are there in all?

- How many are left?
- How many are there altogether?
- How many fewer are there?
- How many more are there?

Adds	Subs

Addison-Wesley | All Rights Reserved

Build the Numbers

Dear Family,
   Your child has been learning about reading and writing 4-digit numbers.
The two of you can learn more about this topic by doing this activity together.

You will need nine index cards or slips of paper. Write each
of the digits 1-9 on a separate card.

Work together or take turns building each of the
following 4-digit numbers.

1. the greatest number _____

2. the least number_____

3. the greatest number with all even digits _____

4. the least number with all odd digits _____

5. the number closest to 5,000 _____

6. the least number with all digits greater than 5 _____

7. the greatest odd number with 7 in the thousands place _____

8. the least even number with 8 in the thousands place _____

9. Build any 4-digit number greater than 2,000. Have your family
   member build a number that is 1,111 less than your number.

10. Build any 4-digit number less than 8,000. See if your family
   member can build a number that is 1,111 greater
   than your number.

Addison-Wesley | All Rights Reserved

Number Puzzle

Complete the puzzle by writing the correct number
for each clue.

Across

1. six hundred fourteen thousand,
   two hundred ninety-seven
5. three hundred twenty-two
6. five hundred twenty-nine
7. four thousand, eighteen
8. twenty
10. ten
11. twenty-seven
12. forty-seven
13. nineteen thousand, six hundred
    thirty-four
16. seven thousand, eight hundred
    twenty
18. seven thousand, four hundred
    thirty-five
19. sixty-two thousand, five
    hundred thirty-one
20. twenty-six
21. fifty-four
22. sixty
23. twelve
24. eight thousand, nine hundred
    fifty

Down

1. six hundred twenty-one
2. one hundred twenty-eight
3. nine hundred fifty-two
4. seven hundred twenty
5. three hundred thousand, nine
   hundred forty-six
7. four hundred eleven thousand,
   seven hundred twenty-nine
9. eight hundred seventy thousand,
   one hundred
11. twenty-four
12. forty-two thousand, three
    hundred sixty-five
14. sixty-three
15. thirty-five
16. seventy-two
17. eighty-five
19. sixty-four

Addison-Wesley | All Rights Reserved

Can You Guess?

Work with a classmate. Think of things you do in the morning, afternoon, and evening. Draw hands on the clockfaces to show the time when you do these things. Have your partner guess what you are doing and record the guesses. Then write the correct answer.

M
O
R
N
I
N
G

_____ _____ _____

_____ _____ _____

A
F
T
E
R
N
O
O
N

_____ _____ _____

_____ _____ _____

E
V
E
N
I
N
G

_____ _____ _____

_____ _____ _____

Addison-Wesley | All Rights Reserved

Sam's A-maze-ing Day

Dear Family,
    In our math book we have just studied telling time to the minute. We also learned about a.m. and p.m. Here is an activity you can do with your child.

Circle a time on the maze below that matches a time on each clockface. Then draw a line from one circle to the next circle to follow Sam's activities throughout the day. Write **a.m.** or **p.m.** next to each time you circle.

	7:01 Exercise	⌒(7:33)⌒———————	8:05 Breakfast
	▬▬▬	▬▬▬	▬▬▬
9:59 Gym	8:53 Homeroom	8:45 First Bell	8:32 School Bus
	▬▬▬	▬▬▬	▬▬▬
10:19 Math	11:08 Science	12:01 Lunch	1:22 Spelling
	▬▬▬	▬▬▬	▬▬▬
7:17 Telephone	6:41 Homework	6:00 Supper	3:16 Sports Program
	▬▬▬	▬▬▬	▬▬▬
8:29 TV	8:43 Reading	9:00 Bedtime	9:40 Snack

Addison-Wesley | All Rights Reserved

The Time It Took

Carla has a paper route. She begins her deliveries at 3:00 p.m.
On Saturday it takes Carla about 5 minutes at each house
because Saturday is collection day.

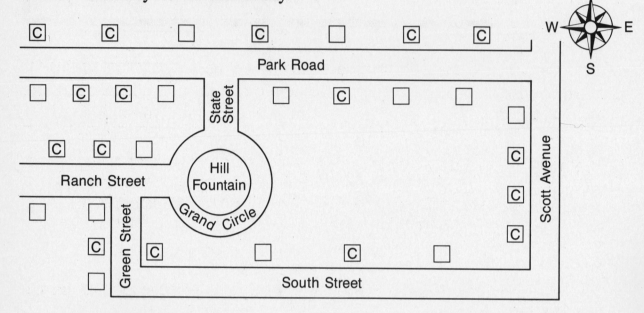

1. It is Saturday. Carla delivers papers only to the houses with a C on
   them. Carla starts at the west end of Park Road. How much time does

   she spend on Park Road? _____ What time is it when

   she reaches Scott Avenue? _____

2. What time is it when Carla finishes deliveries on Scott Avenue and

   arrives at the corner of South Street? _____

3. Where is Carla by 4:05? _____

4. How long does it take Carla to complete her route on Saturday?

   _____ What time does she finish?

   _____

Addison-Wesley | All Rights Reserved

October Days

OCTOBER 2002						
Sunday	Monday	Tuesday	Wednesday	Thursday	Friday	Saturday

1. The first day of October 2002 is a Tuesday. Write the dates for the whole month on the calendar above.

2. Create a symbol for each of these special days. Draw the symbol on the correct date.
Columbus Day: one week after the 5th
Dictionary Day: two days before the 18th
Halloween: four days after the 27th

3. October first is the 274th day of the year. You can write it as 10/1/02. Use numbers to write the date for:

the 278th day _____   the 282nd day _____

the 292nd day _____   the 300th day _____

4. Write the day of the week.

Last day of September 2002   First day of November 2002

_____   _____

Addison-Wesley | All Rights Reserved

How Much Trash?

Solve each problem. Put any
data that you do not need in
the trash can. When you have
completed all the problems,
look in your trash can. Which
data went into the trash?

1. Anita unpacked 12 paper plates
and 15 paper cups for the picnic.
She found 2 plastic spoons on
the table. How many things did
Anita unpack?

_____

2. The treasure hunt started at 2:15
and lasted 1 hour and 15 minutes.
David found 4 clues written in
code. What time was the
treasure hunt over?

_____

3. Mr. Lyons passed out 6 apples,
4 oranges, and 8 plums. Each
piece of fruit cost 39¢. If each
student had 1 piece of fruit,
how many students ate fruit?

_____

4. Nora brought $6 to buy a souvenir.
A button cost $2 and a set of
postcards cost $3. If Nora had
$3 left, what did she buy?

_____

5. By the end of the picnic 35
carrot sticks and 29 celery
sticks had been eaten. Maddy
ate 2 cucumber slices. How
many more carrot sticks than
celery sticks did the group
eat?

_____

6. The students were back at
school by 6:00. The trip took
55 minutes. 23 students rode on
the bus back to school. What
time did the class leave the
picnic grounds?

_____

Addison-Wesley | All Rights Reserved

Fish Fun

Suppose someone gave you a fish tank and you wanted to start keeping fish
in it. Your allowance is $2.75 a week. Check the prices in this pet store.
Decide which things you will need right away and which you can wait to
buy. Calculate what you will buy each week for a month to get your fish
tank started. Use your calculator to help you.

Be sure to write the total amount you spend each week.

Week 1

Item	Price
_____	_____
_____	_____
Total:	_____

Week 2

Item	Price
_____	_____
_____	_____
Total:	_____

Week 3

Item	Price
_____	_____
_____	_____
Total:	_____

Week 4

Item	Price
_____	_____
_____	_____
Total:	_____

Addison-Wesley | All Rights Reserved

A Choice of Cards

The table shows the prices of some baseball cards at
the baseball card owners' meeting.

Homer Runn $1.44	Dave Steve $1.12
Ty Corn $0.75	Kirby Boggs $0.96
Dwayne Badden $1.72	Felix Flyout $0.48

~~Estimate to~~ solve the problems.

1. You have 2 quarters, 4 dimes, and 2 nickels.
Can you buy the Kirby Boggs card?

_____

2. You have 2 quarters, 4 nickels, and 2 pennies.
Can you buy the Ty Corn card?

_____

3. You have 2 quarters and 3 dimes. Which of the
cards can you buy?

_____

4. You have 3 quarters, 4 dimes, 3 nickels, and 2 pennies.
Which of the cards are too expensive for you?

_____

5. You want to buy the Dwayne Badden card. You
have 5 quarters, 2 dimes, and a nickel. Will you
have enough to buy the card if your friend Gary
gives you a quarter?

_____

Addison-Wesley | All Rights Reserved

Name _____

Complete the Cartoons

Dear Family,
    Your child has learned to count change. Use real money to act out with your child the transactions in these cartoons.

Look at each cartoon. Decide what data are missing. Fill in the speech balloon. Tell what the customer says while giving money to the clerk. Or tell what the clerk says while giving change to the customer.

Addison-Wesley | All Rights Reserved

Name _____

Personalized Sweatshirts

You and your friends are going to design personalized sweatshirts for
yourselves. First you have to make some choices. Look at the samples
below and choose the kind of lettering you want for your own initials and
the kind of border you want. Draw your combination on the first sweatshirt
outline. Then ask your friends to choose lettering and a border. Be sure that
no two sweatshirts have the same combinations.

Example:

Lettering	Borders
RJB rjb *RJB*	□X□X□X□X□ ☆☆☆☆☆☆ ♡♡♡♡♡♡

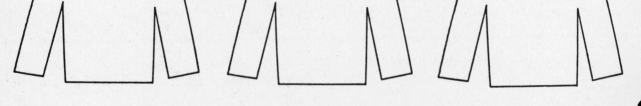

How many other designs can you still make? _____

Addison-Wesley | All Rights Reserved

Number Toss Game

Play the Number Toss game in pairs.

Game Rules
1. Copy and cut out the game board below. Place it on the floor or on a low table.
2. Use a small button or coin for tossing. Stand 3 feet away from the board and take turns tossing the button. Each player gets two tosses a turn.
3. Use mental math to add your 2 scores. Then write the sum on a sheet of paper.
4. The first player to reach a score of 1,000 wins.

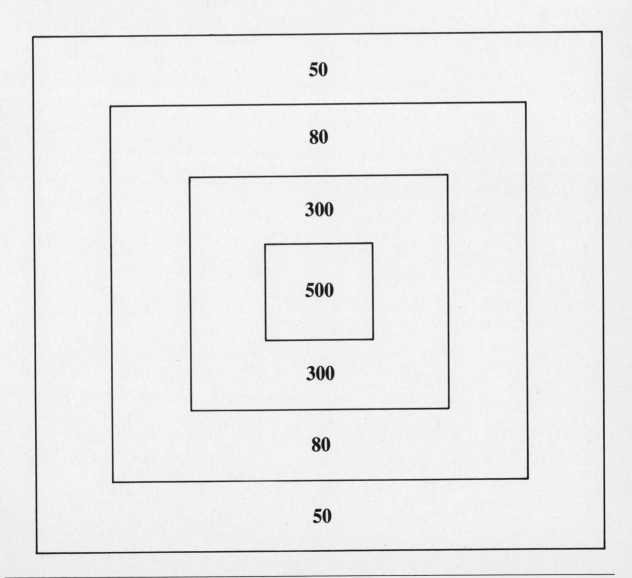

Addison-Wesley | All Rights Reserved

Name _____

School Supplies

Estimate the prices.

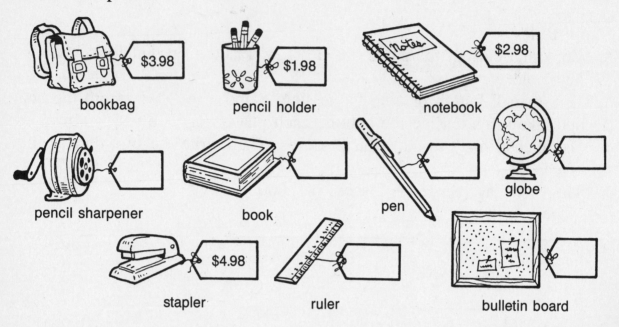

1. Mike bought a pencil holder and a pencil sharpener. He spent about $11. The price of the pencil sharpener is about

_$9_ .

2. Susan bought a bookbag and a book. She spent about $10. The price of the book is about

_____ .

3. Cindy bought a notebook and a globe. She spent about $9. The price of the globe is about

_____ .

4. Mona bought a stapler and a ruler. She spent about $6. The price of the ruler is about

_____ .

5. Jerry bought a stapler and a bulletin board. He spent about $13. The price of the bulletin board is about

_____ .

6. John bought a pencil holder and a pen. He spent about $4. The price of the pen is about

_____ .

Addison-Wesley | All Rights Reserved

Trading Places

Look at each amount. Ring the place value chart in
each row that does *not* belong.

1. 26 ones

A	Tens	Ones
	2	16

B	Tens	Ones
	2	6

C	Tens	Ones
	1	16

2. 24 ones

A	Tens	Ones
	2	4

B	Tens	Ones
	24	

C	Tens	Ones
		24

3. 18 ones

A	Tens	Ones
		18

B	Tens	Ones
	1	8

C	Tens	Ones
	18	8

4. 32 ones

A	Tens	Ones
	30	2

B	Tens	Ones
	3	2

C	Tens	Ones
		32

5. 15 ones

A	Tens	Ones
		15

B	Tens	Ones
	1	5

C	Tens	Ones
	5	1

6. 29 ones

A	Tens	Ones
		29

B	Tens	Ones
	20	9

C	Tens	Ones
	2	9

7. 43 ones

A	Tens	Ones
	3	4

B	Tens	Ones
	4	3

C	Tens	Ones
		43

8. 54 ones

A	Tens	Ones
	5	4

B	Tens	Ones
	54	

C	Tens	Ones
		54

Addison-Wesley | All Rights Reserved

Making Connections

Solve each addition exercise. Find the dot for each answer.
Connect the dots in order from the first answer to the
tenth answer.

1. $\begin{array}{r} 19 \\ + 26 \\ \hline \end{array}$ **2.** $\begin{array}{r} 29 \\ + 33 \\ \hline \end{array}$ **3.** $\begin{array}{r} 48 \\ + 45 \\ \hline \end{array}$ **4.** $\begin{array}{r} 29 \\ + 21 \\ \hline \end{array}$

5. $\begin{array}{r} 19 \\ + 46 \\ \hline \end{array}$ **6.** $\begin{array}{r} 57 \\ + 26 \\ \hline \end{array}$ **7.** $\begin{array}{r} 56 \\ + 35 \\ \hline \end{array}$ **8.** $\begin{array}{r} 24 \\ + 18 \\ \hline \end{array}$

9. $\begin{array}{r} 19 \\ + 15 \\ \hline \end{array}$ **10.** $\begin{array}{r} 43 \\ + 16 \\ \hline \end{array}$

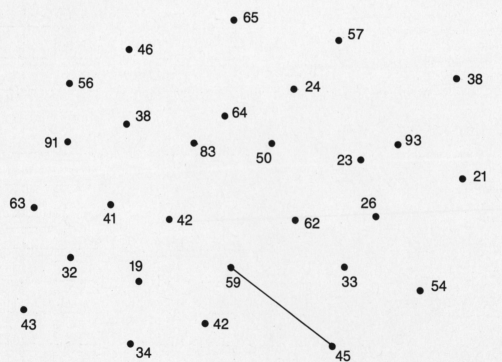

Addison-Wesley | All Rights Reserved

Name

Guess the Rule

Guess each rule. Then write the missing numbers.

1.

Rule: Add 6.	
16	22
24	30
32	38
23	29
35	

2.

Rule:	
26	31
32	37
45	50
38	
62	

3.

Rule:	
18	21
26	29
17	20
43	
58	

4.

Rule:	
44	51
63	70
21	28
55	
92	

5.

Rule:	
38	40
49	51
27	29
90	
78	

6.

Rule:	
73	77
46	50
67	71
58	
12	

7.

Rule:	
32	40
76	84
55	63
43	
18	
21	

8.

Rule:	
17	23
32	38
88	94
66	
55	
44	

9.

Rule:	
46	55
83	92
22	31
53	
14	
37	

Addison-Wesley | All Rights Reserved

Name _____

Check Your Guesses

Robin works at the dog kennel. She likes to learn about dogs. Use the Guess and Check strategy to solve these problems. You may want to use a calculator.

1. Adult dogs have different weights. What 3 dogs total 295 pounds?

English setter	70 pounds
St. Bernard	200 pounds
Siberian husky	60 pounds
Airedale	50 pounds
Basset hound	45 pounds

_____

_____

2. There are 128 breeds of dogs in 7 groups. Use this list. What 2 breeds together total 31?

Herding breeds	14
Hound breeds	21
Terrier breeds	23
Toy breeds	15
Nonsporting breeds	12
Sporting breeds	24
Working breeds	19

_____

_____

3. Use the list in Problem 2. What 2 breeds together total 47?

_____

_____

4. Use the list in Problem 2. What 3 breeds together total 68?

_____

_____

5. Adult dogs have a total of 42 teeth. Which kinds of teeth total 30 teeth?

Front teeth	12
Fangs	4
Molars	26

_____

6. Use the list in Problem 1 to write a problem of your own that can be solved using the strategy Guess and Check.

_____

_____

Addison-Wesley | All Rights Reserved

Missing Numbers

These problems are missing some
numbers. Can you find them?

1.
```
    3 8
+ [ ] 7
─────
    6 5
```

2.
```
    4 2
+ 9 [ ]
─────
  1 4 1
```

3.
```
    5 [ ]
+ [ ] 2
─────
  1 3 8
```

4.
```
  [ ][ ]
+ 6 8
─────
  1 4 3
```

5.
```
    2 3 6
+ [ ][ ] 8
─────
    3 8 4
```

6.
```
  [ ] 5 [ ]
+ 1 9 5
─────
  5 [ ] 7
```

7.
```
    4 7 [ ]
+ 1 [ ] 7
─────
  [ ] 8 3
```

Make your own addition exercises with these sums.
Have a classmate check your exercises.

8.
```
  [ ][ ]
+ [ ][ ]
─────
  1 3 2
```

9.
```
  [ ][ ]
+ [ ][ ]
─────
    7 5
```

10.
```
  [ ][ ]
+   [ ]
─────
    8 0
```

11.
```
  [ ][ ]
+ [ ][ ]
─────
  1 2 6
```

12.
```
  [ ][ ][ ]
+ [ ][ ][ ]
─────
  9 9 2
```

13.
```
  [ ][ ][ ]
+ [ ][ ][ ]
─────
1, 4 2 7
```

Addison-Wesley | All Rights Reserved

Fun with Sums

Numbers such as 1,551, 464, and 81,618 read the same forward and backward. They are called **number palindromes.** You can use addition to find palindromes. Try some. Keep adding until you have a palindrome.

Example:

$$39 \longleftarrow \text{Start with any number.}$$

$$+ 93 \longleftarrow \text{Write the number backward.}$$

$$132 \longleftarrow \text{Add.}$$

$$+ 231 \longleftarrow \text{Write the number backward.}$$

$$363 \longleftarrow \text{The sum is a palindrome.}$$

1.
$$94$$
$$+ 49$$

2.
$$83$$
$$+ 38$$

3.
$$59$$
$$+ 95$$

4.
$$67$$
$$+ 76$$

5.
$$312$$
$$+ 213$$

6.
$$173$$
$$+ 371$$

7.
$$253$$
$$+ 352$$

8.
$$73$$
$$+ 37$$

9.
$$48$$
$$+ 84$$

10.
$$351$$
$$+ 153$$

11.
$$152$$
$$+ 251$$

Addison-Wesley | All Rights Reserved

Name _____

Three Numbers

Write the missing numbers.

1.
4
9
+ [5]
—
18

2.
[ ]
8
+ 6
—
20

3.
7
[ ]
+ 5
—
19

4.
9
6
+ [ ]
—
23

Complete the tables. The sum of the three numbers in each row equals the number shown at the right. The sum of the three numbers in each column equals the number at the bottom.

5.

	5	1	14
7		4	17
1	4	7	12
16	15	12	

6.

3		9	18
			11
4		8	19
12	16	20	

7.

4	6		18
5	7		21
			14
13	15	25	

8.

			21
9		4	18
8		2	17
23	19	14	

Addison-Wesley | All Rights Reserved

Check Your Sums

Dear Family,
   Our class has just studied adding numbers in columns. Try the activity below with your child as a way of checking addition answers.

Study the examples. Then find the sums and use the method shown to check your answers.

Example:

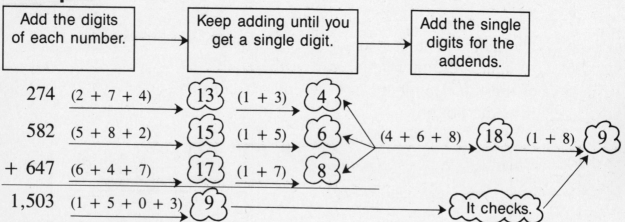

| Add the digits of each number. | Keep adding until you get a single digit. | Add the single digits for the addends. |

1.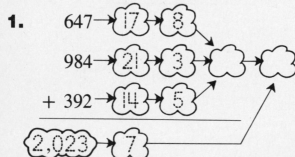

2.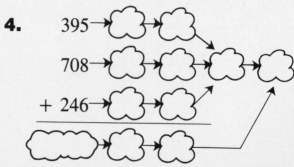

3.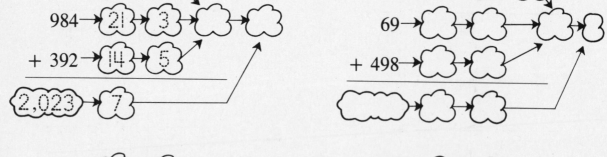

4.

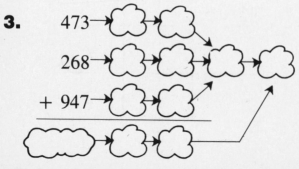

Addison-Wesley | All Rights Reserved

Name _____

Odd and Even Addition

Write **even** digits (0, 2, 4, 6, or 8) in the ◯s.

Write **odd** digits (1, 3, 5, 7, or 9) in the ☐s.

Many different numbers will work. Be sure your addition is correct.

Example:

```
   ④,②  ⑥  ②
+  3, 5  3  1
   7, 7  9  3
```

1.
```
   ◯,◯  ◯  ◯
+  ☐,☐  ☐  ☐
   ☐,☐  ☐  ☐
```

2.
```
   ◯,◯  ◯  ◯
+  ☐,☐  ☐  ☐
   ☐,☐  ◯  ☐
```

3.
```
   ◯,◯  ◯  ◯
+  ☐,☐  ☐  ☐
   ☐,◯  ◯  ☐
```

4.
```
   ◯,◯  ◯  ◯
+  ☐,☐  ☐  ☐
   ◯,☐  ☐  ☐
```

5.
```
   ◯,◯  ◯  ◯
+  ☐,☐  ☐  ☐
   ☐,☐  ☐  ☐
```

6.
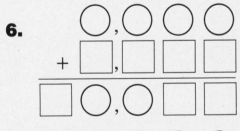

7.
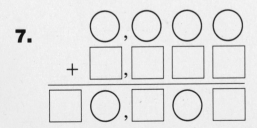

8.
```
   ◯,◯  ◯  ◯
+  ☐,☐  ☐  ☐
   ☐,◯,☐  ☐
```

Addison-Wesley | All Rights Reserved

Bicycle Store

Look at the data about the bicycle store. Write
4 problems that can be answered using the data.
Decide whether you could estimate to find the
correct answer, or if an exact answer is needed.
Then write **estimate** or **exact** for each problem.

Salesperson	Customer 1	Customer 2
Sells about 12 bikes a week.	Bought 1 bike. Wants change from a $100 bill.	Has $40 to spend. Wants to buy a bike.
Needs to reduce prices for a sale.	Wants to compare the difference in prices.	Bought 2 small headlights. Needs to figure out the total cost.

1. Problem: _____

_____

_____

Answer: _____

3. Problem: _____

_____

_____

Answer: _____

2. Problem: _____

_____

_____

Answer: _____

4. Problem: _____

_____

_____

Answer: _____

Addison-Wesley | All Rights Reserved

Name _____

Sam's Spending Spree

Sam received a total of $20.00 for his birthday. Look at this catalog page. Help Sam spend his money on parts for his model railroad. Solve the problems. Compare your answers to a partner's.

Tree	$ 1.15	Mountain tunnel	$17.30
Gas station	$ 4.60	Telephone poles, each	$ 1.50
Bank	$ 5.40	Curved track, each	$ 3.00
Shrub	$ 0.70	Straight track, each	$ 2.00
Caboose	$17.00	Railroad crossing sign	$ 2.10

1. How much would it cost Sam to buy both the mountain tunnel and 1 tree?

_____

2. What would it cost Sam to buy 1 bank and 2 straight tracks?

_____

3. What item could Sam buy the most of?

_____

the fewest of? _____

4. If Sam buys 3 curved tracks and 2 straight tracks, how much money will he have left?

_____

Use the data in the catalog to make up two of your own problems. Then have your partner solve them.

5. _____

_____

_____

6. _____

_____

_____

Addison-Wesley | All Rights Reserved

Balloon Race

Find the differences. Write the answer next to each balloon.

1.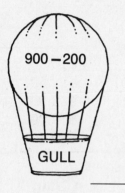

900 − 200

GULL

_____

2.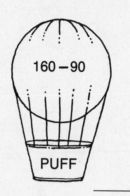

160 − 90

PUFF

_____

3.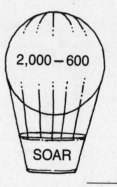

2,000 − 600

SOAR

_____

4.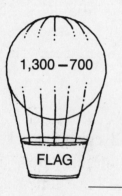

1,300 − 700

FLAG

_____

5.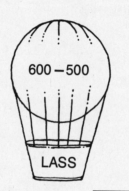

600 − 500

LASS

_____

6.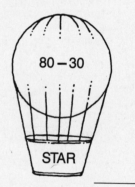

80 − 30

STAR

_____

7.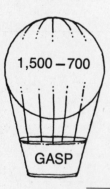

1,500 − 700

GASP

_____

8.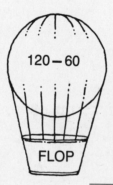

120 − 60

FLOP

_____

9.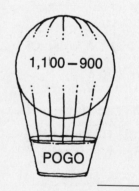

1,100 − 900

POGO

_____

Addison-Wesley | All Rights Reserved

Addison-Wesley | All Rights Reserved

Name _____

~~Estimating~~ Exact Savings

Sammy Savesalot loves a good sale. Help Sammy out.
Fill in ~~about~~ **how much** he would save on the items below
if he bought them on sale. ~~Round to the nearest ten or hundred.~~

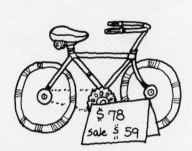

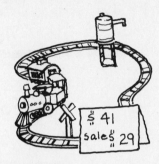

1. Sammy would save

~~about~~ _____.

2. He would save

~~about~~ _____.

3. He would save

~~about~~ _____.

4. He would save

~~about~~ _____.

5. He would save

~~about~~ _____.

6. He would save

~~about~~ _____.

7. He would save

~~about~~ _____.

8. He would save

~~about~~ _____.

9. He would save

~~about~~ _____.

Fair Trades

Dear Family,
   Play this trading game with your child. Have your child toss a coin. If the coin lands on heads, your child makes the first trade in Column A. If the coin lands on tails, the first trade is made in Column B. Take turns until all the trades have been made.

A

Trade 1 ten for 10 ones.

Example:

89 ___ 7 tens, 19 ones ___

1. 22 _____
2. 57 _____
3. 74 _____
4. 36 _____
5. 65 _____
6. 97 _____
7. 20 _____
8. 16 _____
9. 71 _____
10. 45 _____

B

Trade 10 ones for 1 ten.

Example:

6 tens, 17 ones ___ 77 ___

1. 4 tens, 11 ones ___
2. 2 tens, 14 ones ___
3. 3 tens, 10 ones ___
4. 7 tens, 18 ones ___
5. 5 tens, 12 ones ___
6. 1 ten, 19 ones ___
7. 6 tens, 13 ones ___
8. 9 tens, 10 ones ___
9. 8 tens, 16 ones ___
10. 0 tens, 17 ones ___

Addison-Wesley | All Rights Reserved

Check the Quiz

Someone completed this quiz in a hurry. Help the
student correct any mistakes. Identify each error.
Then rewrite the exercise so the answer is correct.
Use place value blocks to help you check.

1.
$$\begin{array}{r} 81 \\ -\ 46 \\ \hline 34 \end{array}$$

2.
$$\begin{array}{r} 66 \\ -\ 59 \\ \hline 7 \end{array}$$

3.
$$\begin{array}{r} 28 \\ -\ 19 \\ \hline 7 \end{array}$$

4.
$$\begin{array}{r} 42 \\ -\ 27 \\ \hline 25 \end{array}$$

5.
$$\begin{array}{r} 34 \\ -\ 17 \\ \hline 17 \end{array}$$

6.
$$\begin{array}{r} 53 \\ -\ 36 \\ \hline 16 \end{array}$$

7.
$$\begin{array}{r} 31 \\ -\ 25 \\ \hline 16 \end{array}$$

8.
$$\begin{array}{r} 72 \\ -\ 49 \\ \hline 13 \end{array}$$

9.
$$\begin{array}{r} 65 \\ -\ 26 \\ \hline 38 \end{array}$$

10.
$$\begin{array}{r} 57 \\ -\ 18 \\ \hline 39 \end{array}$$

11.
$$\begin{array}{r} 22 \\ -\ 6 \\ \hline 28 \end{array}$$

12.
$$\begin{array}{r} 45 \\ -\ 38 \\ \hline 7 \end{array}$$

13. How many exercises did you correct? _____

Addison-Wesley | All Rights Reserved

Subtracting Even and Odd Digits

Write **even** digits (0, 2, 4, 6, or 8) in the ◯s.

Write **odd** digits (1, 3, 5, 7, or 9) in the ☐s.

Many different numbers will work. Be sure your subtraction is correct.

Examples:

$$
\begin{array}{r}
②\ ☐1 \\
-\ \ ④ \\
\hline
☐1\ ☐7
\end{array}
\qquad
\begin{array}{r}
☐1\ ☐9 \\
-\ \ ☐3 \\
\hline
☐1\ ⑥
\end{array}
\qquad
\begin{array}{r}
☐3\ ④ \\
-\ ☐1\ ⑧ \\
\hline
☐1\ ⑥
\end{array}
$$

1.

2.

3.

4.

5.

6.

7.

8.

9.

10.

11.

12.

13.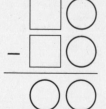

14.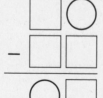

15.

16.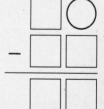

Addison-Wesley | All Rights Reserved

Working with Tables

Complete the table below and then solve the problem.

1. Lynn belongs to a book club. Every time she buys 4 books from the book club, she gets 5 bonus points. When she has 25 points, she gets a free book. How many books does she have to buy to get a free one?

_____

Books bought	4				
Bonus points	5	10	15	20	25

Write a paragraph that explains how you solved the problem by completing the table.

_____

_____

_____

_____

2. Write a word problem using information in this table.

Number of stickers	6	12	18	24
Number of pages	1	2	3	4

_____

_____

Addison-Wesley | All Rights Reserved

Name _____

Tall Buildings

The table shows the heights of some tall buildings around the country.

Building	City	Height in Feet
First National Bank	Boston	591
IBM Tower	Atlanta	825
Renaissance Center	Detroit	479
Republic Plaza	Denver	714
Texas Commerce Tower	Dallas	738
TransAmerica Pyramid	San Francisco	853
Pillsbury Center	Minneapolis	561

Use the information in the table to solve the problems.

1. What is the difference in height between the First National Bank and the IBM tower?

_____

2. Which building is 262 feet shorter than the TransAmerica Pyramid?

_____

3. Which building is 153 feet shorter than the Republic Plaza?

_____

4. Which building is 115 feet shorter than the TransAmerica Pyramid?

_____

5. Which two buildings have a difference in height of 112 feet?

_____

Addison-Wesley | All Rights Reserved

A Double Difference

Many 3-digit numbers have a double difference.
The double difference is a 2-digit number.

You can use subtraction to find the double difference.
Work with a partner to analyze the examples.

Examples:

419 ⟵	Start with a number that has ⟶	297
	three different digits.	
914 ⟵	Reverse the digits. ⟶	792

$$
\begin{array}{r} 914 \\ -419 \\ \hline 495 \end{array}
\quad\longleftarrow\quad \text{Find the difference.} \quad\longrightarrow\quad
\begin{array}{r} 792 \\ -297 \\ \hline 495 \end{array}
$$

495 ⟵	Take the answer. ⟶	495
594 ⟵	Reverse the digits. ⟶	594

$$
\begin{array}{r} 594 \\ -495 \\ \hline 99 \end{array}
\quad\longleftarrow\quad \text{Find the difference.} \quad\longrightarrow\quad
\begin{array}{r} 594 \\ -495 \\ \hline 99 \end{array}
$$

Work with your partner to find the double difference
for each number. Take turns reversing the digits
and finding the difference. Check each other's answers.

1. 712   **2.** 843   **3.** 176   **4.** 754   **5.** 417

Addison-Wesley | All Rights Reserved

Raindrops Are Falling

Raindrops fell on these exercises. Rewrite the
exercises so that the hidden numbers can be seen.

1.
$$\begin{array}{r} \bigcirc \\ -\ 219 \\ \hline 165 \end{array}$$

2.
$$\begin{array}{r} 821 \\ -\ \bigcirc \\ \hline 601 \end{array}$$

3.
$$\begin{array}{r} 724 \\ -\ 1\bigcirc \\ \hline 569 \end{array}$$

4.
$$\begin{array}{r} 829 \\ -\ 44\bigcirc \\ \hline \bigcirc 5 \end{array}$$

5.
$$\begin{array}{r} 919 \\ -\bigcirc 58 \\ \hline 261 \end{array}$$

6.
$$\begin{array}{r} 508 \\ -\ \bigcirc \\ \hline 321 \end{array}$$

7.
$$\begin{array}{r} \bigcirc \\ -\ 677 \\ \hline 39 \end{array}$$

8.
$$\begin{array}{r} \bigcirc 91 \\ -\ 103 \\ \hline 588 \end{array}$$

9.
$$\begin{array}{r} 2\bigcirc 5 \\ -\ 106 \\ \hline 129 \end{array}$$

10.
$$\begin{array}{r} 312 \\ -\ 18\bigcirc \\ \hline 132 \end{array}$$

11.
$$\begin{array}{r} \bigcirc \\ -\ 222 \\ \hline 431 \end{array}$$

12.
$$\begin{array}{r} 913 \\ -\ \bigcirc \\ \hline 528 \end{array}$$

Addison-Wesley | All Rights Reserved

Name _____

Check Your Differences

Analyze the examples. Then find the differences. Use the
method shown to check your answers.

Example:

| Add the digits of each number. | → | Keep adding until you get a single digit. | → | Add the single digits from the bottom two numbers. |

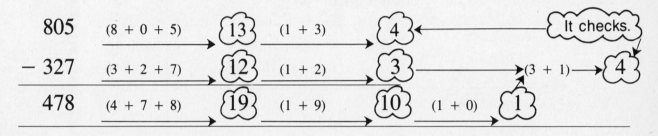

							It checks.
805	(8 + 0 + 5)	⑬	(1 + 3)	④	←		
− 327	(3 + 2 + 7)	⑫	(1 + 2)	③	→	(3 + 1) → ④	
478	(4 + 7 + 8)	⑲	(1 + 9)	⑩	(1 + 0) → ①		

1.

904 → ⑬ → ④ ←
− 267 → ⑮ → ⑥ → ⑬ →
637 → ⑯ → ⑦

2.

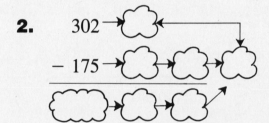

302 →
− 175 →

3.

709 →
− 483 →

4.

605 →
− 526 →

5.

400 →
− 201 →

6.

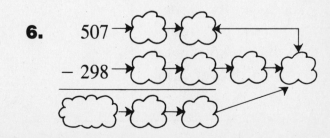

507 →
− 298 →

Addison-Wesley | All Rights Reserved

Name _____

Better Bargains

Dear Family,
   Your child has been developing skills in subtraction. Some exercises with estimating and finding differences are given below. Observe as your child completes the chart. Further practice in subtracting with amounts of money at home will benefit your child's progress in math.

Read the problems. Then complete the chart.

Problem	Estimate	Exact Difference	Was the estimate high or low?
How much money will you save by buying white shoelaces at $0.98 instead of striped ones at $2.79?			
What is the savings if you order a $4.81 dinner instead of the $8.18 Super Special?			
How much can you save by going to the afternoon show at $2.80 instead of the evening show at $3.50?			
What do you save by buying a paperback book at $3.60 instead of a hardcover book at $12.99?			

Addison-Wesley | All Rights Reserved

A Special Book Sale

Claws and Paws Bookshop sells only books that are interesting to animals because animals are their only customers. Today they are having a big sale on their most popular books.

Fill in the missing information on each price tag.

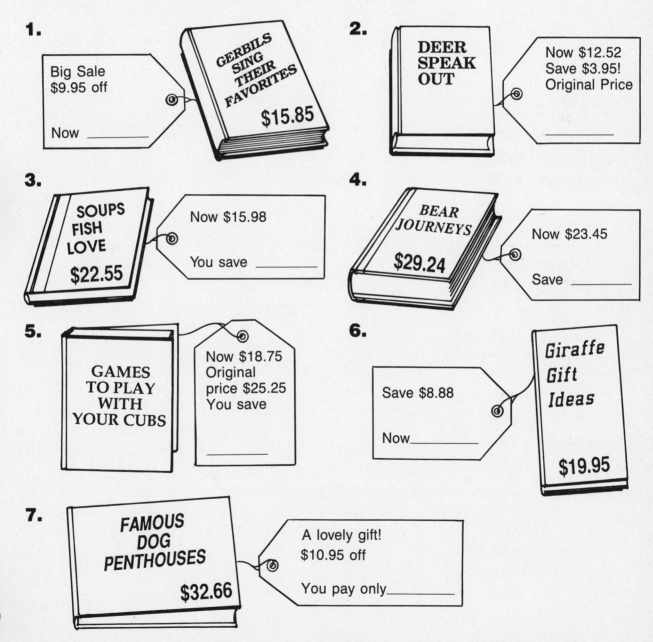

1.

Big Sale
$9.95 off

Now _____

GERBILS SING THEIR FAVORITES

$15.85

2.

DEER SPEAK OUT

Now $12.52
Save $3.95!
Original Price

_____

3.

SOUPS FISH LOVE

$22.55

Now $15.98

You save _____

4.

BEAR JOURNEYS

$29.24

Now $23.45

Save _____

5.

GAMES TO PLAY WITH YOUR CUBS

Now $18.75
Original price $25.25
You save

_____

6.

Save $8.88

Now_____

Giraffe Gift Ideas

$19.95

7.

FAMOUS DOG PENTHOUSES

$32.66

A lovely gift!
$10.95 off

You pay only_____

Addison-Wesley | All Rights Reserved

Name _____

Path Problems

Complete the paths. Choose a calculation method to solve each step along the way.

1. Start

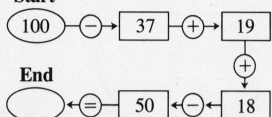

2. Start
End

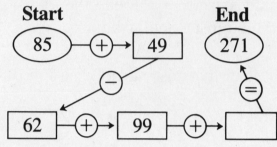

3. Start

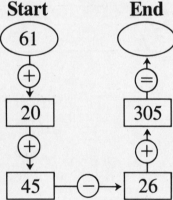

4. Start

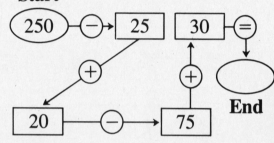

5. Start   End

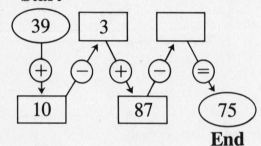

6. Start

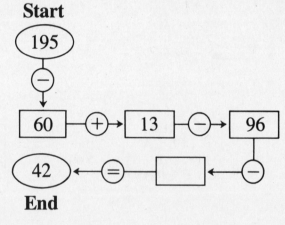

Write a path problem for a friend to complete.

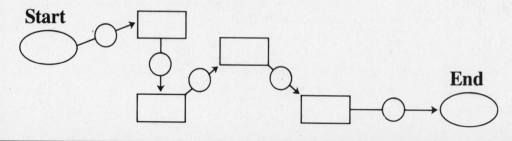

Addison-Wesley | All Rights Reserved

Name _____

How Much Is Left?

Mary, Henry, and Kim had a rummage sale.

	Mary	Henry	Kim
Games	checkers $3.05	cube $1.25	puzzle $0.75
Toys	train $3.19	tractor $1.39	yo-yo $0.89
Balls	soccer ball $3.15	football $1.35	softball $0.85

1. You want to buy one game, one toy, and one ball. You also want to buy only one thing from each person. You have $6 to spend. What can you buy? Write your choices. How much money will be left after you buy all three items?

	Item	Amount
Game:	_____	_____
Toy:	_____	_____
Ball:	_____	_____

Total spent: _____ Change: _____

2. Now pick three other items.

	Item	Amount
Game:	_____	_____
Toy:	_____	_____
Ball:	_____	_____

Total spent: _____ Change: _____

3. Try it once more.

	Item	Amount
Game:	_____	_____
Toy:	_____	_____
Ball:	_____	_____

Total spent: _____ Change: _____

Addison-Wesley | All Rights Reserved

The Way We Go

Look at the bar graph. Then write the answers.

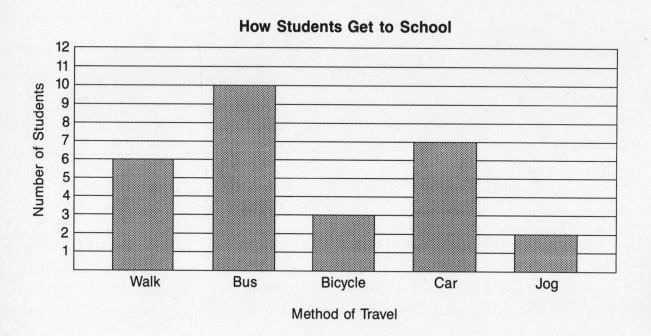

How Students Get to School

1. How many students ride bicycles to school? _____

2. How do most students in the class get to school? _____

3. The graph shows that _____ students use wheels to get to school.

Write two questions of your own using data shown on the graph. Have a classmate answer your questions.

_____

_____

_____

_____

Use with text pages 158–159.

CS-3

Addison-Wesley | All Rights Reserved

Name _____

Tally Time

The customers in a restaurant are telling what their favorite foods are. Work with a classmate to organize data in a tally chart. One person counts a particular food and marks tallies on a chart. Each of you counts and tallies three foods.

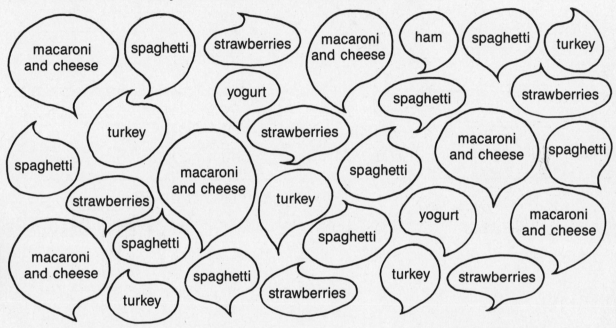

Take turns answering the questions.

1. What was the most popular

food? _____

2. How many people chose

turkey? _____

3. What foods were chosen the same

number of times? _____

_____

Favorite Foods

Food	Choices

Addison-Wesley | All Rights Reserved

Find Rupert's Mistakes

Rupert made a table of the number
of animals he saw in a magic show.

Animals in the Magic Show	
rabbits	23
birds	11
lions	1
frogs	17
snakes	7

Rupert used data from the table to make the bar graph below.
However, Rupert made mistakes. Identify each mistake and ring it.

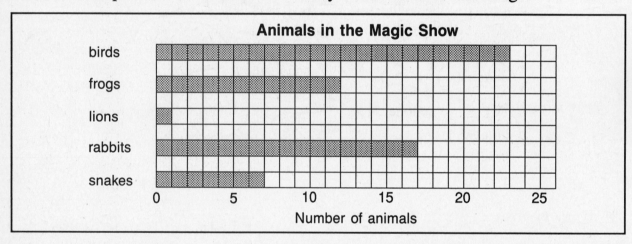

Do Rupert's graph over for him. Use the empty graph below.
Be careful not to make the same mistakes Rupert made.

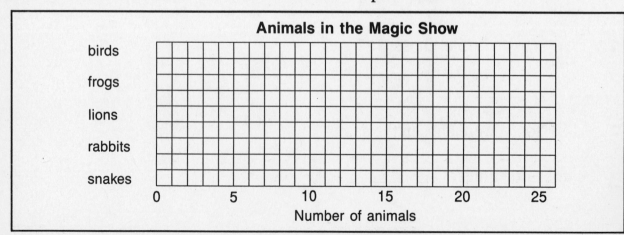

Addison-Wesley | All Rights Reserved

Making a Picture Graph

Event	Tickets
School Band	45
School Play	35
Winter Carnival	55
Magic Night	40
Spring Show	60

Color Ticket s and parts of Ticket s to show the number of tickets sold for each event.

Each Ticket means 10 tickets.

Event	Number of tickets sold					
School Band	Ticket	Ticket	Ticket	Ticket	Ticket	Ticket
School Play	Ticket	Ticket	Ticket	Ticket	Ticket	Ticket
Winter Carnival	Ticket	Ticket	Ticket	Ticket	Ticket	Ticket
Magic Night	Ticket	Ticket	Ticket	Ticket	Ticket	Ticket
Spring Show	Ticket	Ticket	Ticket	Ticket	Ticket	Ticket

1. If 15 more tickets had been sold for the School Play, how many Ticket s in all would be colored for that event? _____

2. How many more Ticket s were colored for the Winter Carnival than for the School Band? _____

3. The number of tickets sold for the School Sing was twice the number sold for Magic Night. How many Ticket s would have to be colored in for the School Sing? _____

Addison-Wesley | All Rights Reserved

Number Words

Use the chart to figure out the numbers for the words.
You may want to use a calculator.

A = 1	B = 2	C = 3	D = 4	E = 5
F = 6	G = 7	H = 8	I = 9	J = 10
K = 11	L = 12	M = 13	N = 14	O = 15
P = 16	Q = 17	R = 18	S = 19	T = 20
U = 21	V = 22	W = 23	X = 24	Y = 25
Z = 26				

1. Write a three-letter word whose number is greater than 6.

_____ _____ _____

2. Write a four-letter word whose number is less than 30.

_____ _____ _____ _____

3. Write a three-letter word whose number is less than 10.

_____ _____ _____

4. Write a four-letter word whose number is greater than 12.

_____ _____ _____ _____

5. Write a four-letter word whose number is less than 75.

_____ _____ _____ _____

6. Write a five-letter word whose number is greater than 40.

_____ _____ _____ _____ _____

7. Write a four-letter word that gives a total of exactly 42.

_____ _____ _____ _____

Addison-Wesley | All Rights Reserved

What Is the Rule?

Study the pattern to complete each table. Then identify the rule.

1.

In	Out
1	5
2	6
3	7
4	___
5	___
6	___

Rule: _____

2.

In	Out
1	4
2	6
3	8
4	___
5	___
6	___

Rule: _____

_____

3.

In	Out
1	5
2	4
3	7
4	6
5	___
6	___
7	___

Rule: _____

_____

4.

In	Out
4	6
5	4
6	8
7	6
8	___
9	___
___	___

Rule: _____

_____

Addison-Wesley | All Rights Reserved

Special Days

Students, teachers, and parents at Bradley School were asked how many special events should be held at school during one school year. The list shows data from the survey.

Students	Teachers	Parents
5	1	2
5	2	0
3	2	4
4	1	1
5	4	2
3	3	1
3	1	3
1	2	3
5	2	5
5	3	3

1. Use the data to complete the table.

Number of Special Events in a School Year

Number of Events	0	1	2	3	4	5
Students						

Use the data from the table to draw conclusions.

2. What can you conclude about how students feel?

_____

_____

3. What can you conclude about how all three groups

feel about having no special events? _____

_____

4. How many special events would make the greatest number

of people happy? _____ Why? _____

_____

Addison-Wesley | All Rights Reserved

Places in the Park

Dear Family,
   Play this probability game with your child. One person uses Spinner 1 and the other uses Spinner 2. Each player spins 48 times. Use the chart below to keep a record of how many times you visit each place.

Rules:
1. Each player begins at **Start** and moves to the first box on the path. Each player then spins to find out whether to turn left or right.
2. Each in turn follows that path to the next box. Spin again to find out which way to turn.
3. Keep spinning and moving to the next box until you reach a place in the park. Make a mark in the chart to show the place you visited. Then start again.
4. The player who visits the most places wins.

paper fastener Spinner 1 Left/Right	Spinner 2 Left Right	
Number of Visits		
Place	Spinner 1	Spinner 2
Picnic Area		
Boat Pond		
Swings		
Sandbox		
Jungle Gym		
Snack Bar		
Ball Field		
Tennis Court		

Analyze the chart and compare the results for Spinner 1 to the results for Spinner 2. Is the game fair or unfair?

Addison-Wesley | All Rights Reserved

Follow the Line

Study the data on the line graphs. Use the data to predict
answers to each question.

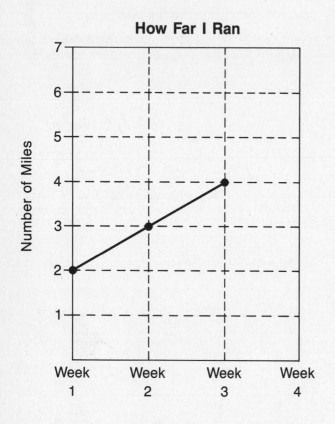

How Far I Ran

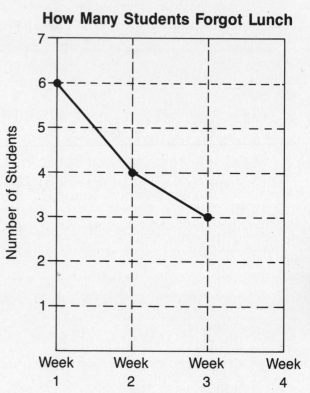

How Many Students Forgot Lunch

1. Delia is training for a race. She
made a line graph to show how
far she ran each week. Do you
predict that the line on the graph
will go up or down in Week 4?

_____

Why? _____

_____

_____

2. This graph shows how many
students in Grade 3 forgot to
bring their lunch during the first
three weeks of school. Do you
predict that the line on the graph
will go up or down in Week 4?

_____

Why? _____

_____

_____

Addison-Wesley | All Rights Reserved

Name _____

Party Time

Dear Family,
    Our math class has been using calculators to solve problems. The
problems below will give your child a chance to share these skills with you.

Use a calculator to solve the problems.

1. The Partytime Company made 1,609 pinwheels in April and 1,901 in May. How many does it need to make to have 5,500

   by the end of June? _____

2. Partytime has 5,000 balloons ready to send to stores. It sends 1,900 to the Eastern Region, 1,200 to the West, and 895 to the Middle West. How many does it have left

   for the South? _____

3. The Partytime Company also makes noisemakers. The first year it made 870, the second year it made 1,750, and the third year it made 2,490. If the company makes 3,200 noisemakers next year, how many will it have made

   altogether? _____

4. Partytime specializes in 4 types of hats. The company has made 9,490 hats. It has made 2,910 pirate hats, 2,085 magician hats, 1,075 witch hats, and clown hats. How many clown hats has

   the company made? _____

Addison-Wesley | All Rights Reserved

Inch Search

Estimate each line length. Check your estimates
by measuring to the nearest inch.

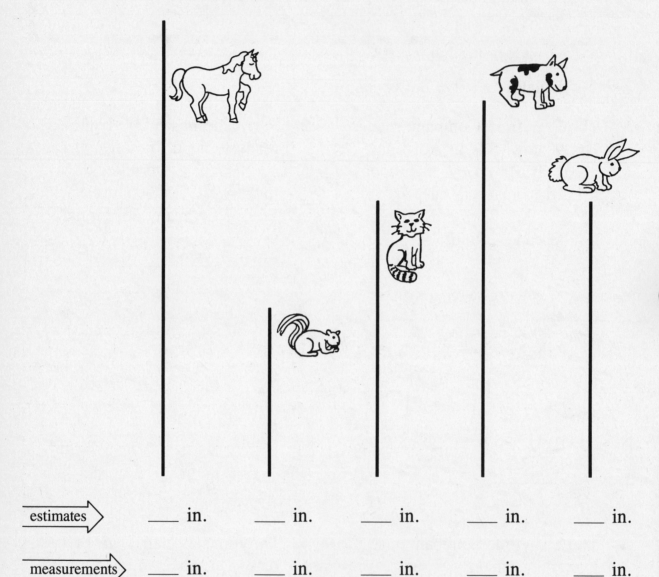

estimates ⟩ ___ in.   ___ in.   ___ in.   ___ in.   ___ in.

measurements ⟩ ___ in.   ___ in.   ___ in.   ___ in.   ___ in.

Follow the directions.

1. Ring the animal that is on the longest line.

2. Mark an X on the animal that is on the shortest line.

3. Find the 2 lines that are of equal length. Draw a line to
    connect the two animals at the ends of these lines.

Addison-Wesley | All Rights Reserved

Name

Inch Along

Dear Family,
   Your child has just studied estimating lengths by using a benchmark such as a paper clip. The activity below gives your child a chance to share this skill with you.

There are two line paths from **Start** to **Finish**. Guess whose path is shorter. First choose a benchmark. Use a ruler to measure your benchmark to the nearest inch. Then estimate the length of each path with the benchmark.

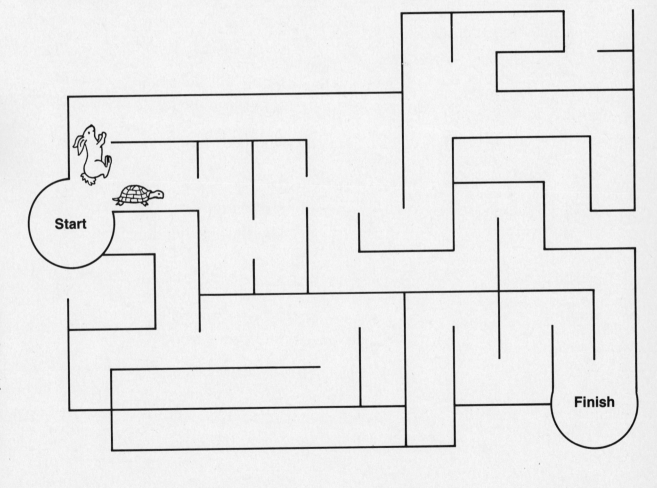

 about _____ inches   about _____ inches

The _____ path is shorter.

Addison-Wesley | All Rights Reserved

Lengthy Units

Complete this chart. Write in the missing units of length.

> **Remember:**
> 1 foot = 12 in.
> 1 yard = 36 in.
> = 3 ft

1.

Feet	1	2	3	4	5	6
Inches						

2.

Yards	1	2	3	4	5	6
Feet						

3.

Yards	1	2	3	4	5	6
Inches						

Decide on the best unit for measuring each item.
Write **inches**, **feet**, or **miles**.

> **Remember:**
> 1 mile = 5,280 ft

4. length of a hairbrush

_____

5. width of an ocean

_____

6. height of a ceiling

_____

7. length of a window

_____

8. height of a drinking glass

_____

9. distance from New York to Florida

_____

List 3 items to measure. Write an item for each of
these units of length: inches, feet, and miles.

10. length of a _____ measure in _____

11. height of a _____ measure in _____

12. distance from _____ to _____ measure in _____

Addison-Wesley | All Rights Reserved

Missing Lengths

Find the missing lengths. Use the perimeters to help you.

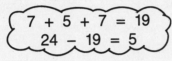

1.

7 in.

5 in. _5_ in.

7 in.

Perimeter = 24 in.

2.

8 in. 8 in.

___ in.

Perimeter = 24 in.

3.

2 ft

___ ft 8 ft

2 ft

Perimeter = 20 ft

4.

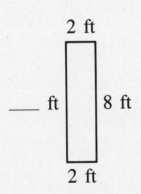

3 ft 5 ft

___ ft

Perimeter = 12 ft

5.

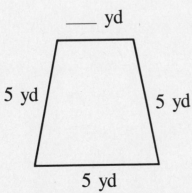

___ yd

5 yd 5 yd

5 yd

Perimeter = 18 yd

6.

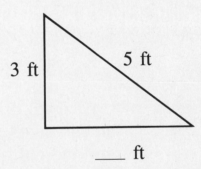

3 yd

3 yd 3 yd

___ yd 3 yd

___ yd

Perimeter = 18 yd

Addison-Wesley | All Rights Reserved

Name _____

Stars and Stripes

Answer the questions below about the American flag.

1. In 1777, the first U.S. flag had between 7 and 15 stars. It had more than 11 stars. The number of stars was an odd number. How many stars did this flag have? _____

2. The flag of 1777 lasted fewer than 19 years and more than 16. It lasted for an odd number of years. How many years did the flag of 1777 last? _____

3. The flag of 1861 had an even number of stars between 32 and 42. It had fewer than 36 stars. How many stars did the flag of 1861 have? _____

4. The flag of 1912 lasted between 41 years and 49 years. It lasted for an odd number of years. It lasted for over 43 years. It did not last for 45 years. How many years did the flag of 1912 last? _____

5. Today's U.S. flag has more stars than the 1912 flag. The 1912 flag had 48 stars. Today's flag also has an even number of stars. It has fewer than 52 stars. How many stars does today's flag have? _____

6. Today's flag has an odd number of stripes. It has 7 red stripes and an even number of white stripes. The white stripes are more than 4 but fewer than 8. How many white stripes are there? _____

Addison-Wesley | All Rights Reserved

Name _____

To Measure or to Estimate

Decide whether you need an estimate (**E**) or an exact measurement (**M**) for each problem.

_____ **1.** how much paper to buy to cover a large bulletin board

_____ **2.** how tall to make each letter for the bulletin board title so they are all the same size

_____ **3.** how many stickers you might need to decorate a book cover

_____ **4.** how many pencils you will need to do schoolwork for a month

_____ **5.** how big to cut paper to cover a window

_____ **6.** how many packs of paper you will use to do homework in a year

_____ **7.** how many times you will sharpen your pencil before it is too small to use

_____ **8.** how big to cut paper to wrap a present

_____ **9.** how big to cut paper to cover the bulletin board exactly

_____ **10.** how big your foot is for buying new shoes

Addison-Wesley | All Rights Reserved

Name _____

Does It Balance?

1 pound   1 ounce   5 ounces

Remember:
16 ounces = 1 pound

Does the scale balance? Ring **yes** or **no**.

1.

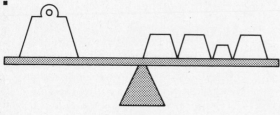

yes   no

2.

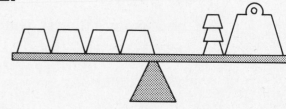

yes   no

3.

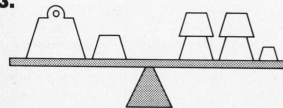

yes   no

4.

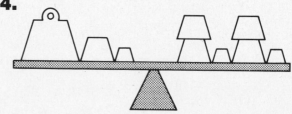

yes   no

5.

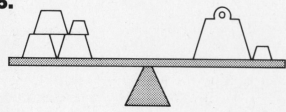

yes   no

6.

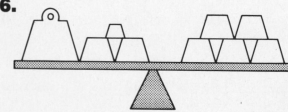

yes   no

Addison-Wesley | All Rights Reserved

Ring the Bell

Answer each question about capacity. Then
write the answers in the boxes under the bell,
beginning at the bottom.

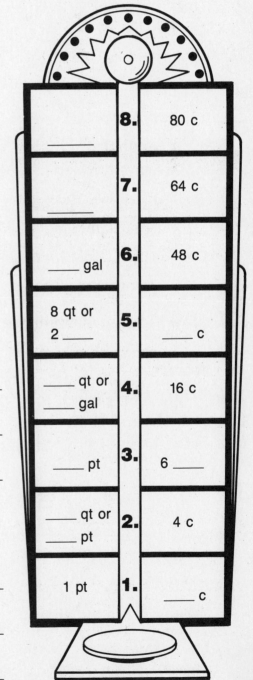

Remember:
2 cups (c) = 1 pint (p)
4 c = 2 pt = 1 quart (qt)
4 qt = 1 gallon (gal)

1. How many cups equal 1 pint? _____

2. 4 cups equal _____ quart or _____ pints.

3. _____ pints equal 6 _____ .

4. 16 cups equal _____ gallon or _____ quarts.

5. _____ cups equal 2 _____ or 8 quarts.

6. 48 cups equal _____ gallons.

7. Write your own problems for 64 cups. Then fill in the box to ring the bell.

_____

_____

_____

8. Write your own problem for 80 cups. Then fill in the box to ring the bell.

_____

_____

Bell diagram (top to bottom, left column then right column):

Left column: _____ | _____ | _____ gal | 8 qt or 2 _____ | _____ qt or _____ gal | _____ pt | _____ qt or _____ pt | 1 pt

Right column: **8.** 80 c | **7.** 64 c | **6.** 48 c | **5.** _____ c | **4.** 16 c | **3.** 6 _____ | **2.** 4 c | **1.** _____ c

Addison-Wesley | All Rights Reserved

Chart the Data

Work with a partner to complete the chart. Visit your school
library and your neighborhood library to gather the data you need.

Facts About Our Libraries	School Library	Neighborhood Library
Year Opened	_____	_____
Number of children's mysteries	_____	_____
Number of children's magazines	_____	_____
Number of children's biographies	_____	_____
Number of librarians	_____	_____

Work with your partner to write 2 problems. Use the data
from the chart. Then exchange papers with two other
classmates and solve the problems.

1. _____   2. _____

_____   _____

_____   _____

_____   _____

Answer: _____   Answer: _____

Addison-Wesley | All Rights Reserved

Writing Problems

Write numbers in the problems so that the
given answers are correct.

Example:

Juan played soccer for __2__ hours each
day. He played for __3__ days. How
many hours did he play in all?

Answer: 6 hours

There is more than one right way to complete
each problem.

1. Sue scored _____ points in the

first game. She scored _____
points in the second game. How
many points did she score in
the two games?

Answer: 15

2. Ben had _____ tickets to sell.

He sold _____ tickets the first
day. How many does he have
left to sell?

Answer: 8

3. Betty bought _____ tickets.

Each ticket cost _____ . How
much did she pay for the
tickets?

Answer: $18

4. Tony rode _____ miles one day.

He rode _____ miles the next
day. How much farther did he
ride the first day?

Answer: 3 miles

Addison-Wesley | All Rights Reserved

Name _____

Add and Multiply

Work with a partner. Draw objects to illustrate these sets.
Then write an addition equation and a multiplication
equation for each drawing.

1. Two threes

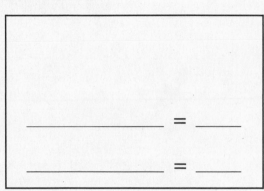

2. Two sixes

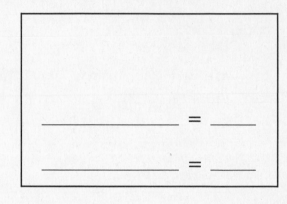

3. Four fives

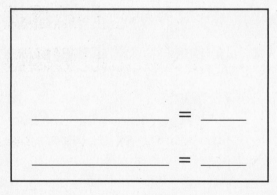

4. Five twos

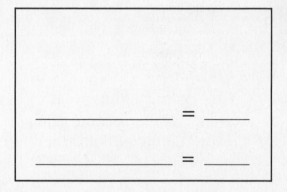

Make up your own addition and multiplication equation for
each box. Draw pictures to illustrate them.

5.

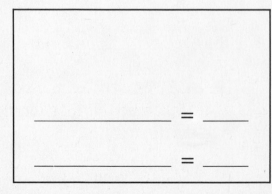

6.

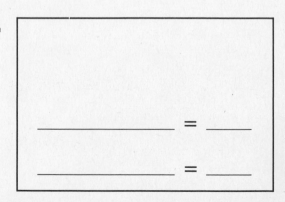

Addison-Wesley | All Rights Reserved

Name _____

How Many Twos?

Write three facts about twos for each picture.

1.

$$2 \times 2 = 4 \qquad 3 \times 2 = 6$$
white circles   black circles

$$5 \times 2 = 10$$
all circles

2.

_____   _____
white circles   black circles

_____
all circles

3.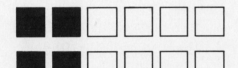

_____   _____
black squares   white squares

_____
all squares

4.

_____   _____
white squares   black squares

_____
all squares

5.

_____   _____
white triangles   black triangles

_____
all triangles

Addison-Wesley | All Rights Reserved

Who Am I?

Use the clues to solve the riddles.

1.

I am double the product of
4 × 5. When you skip count
in this pattern, I am the second
number after 30:

   20, 25, 30, _____, _____.

Who am I?

_____

2.

When you subtract 5 from
the product of 4 × 5, I am
that number.

Who am I?

_____

3.

When you skip count by
fives, I am the number you
count after 30.

Who am I?

_____

4.

Find the product of 5 and 5.
When you add another 5 to the
product, I am that number.

Who am I?

_____

5.

When you subtract 5 from the
product of 10 × 5, I am that
number.

Who am I?

_____

6.

I am the product of two odd
numbers that are the same.
The sum of my digits is 7.

Who am I?

_____

Addison-Wesley | All Rights Reserved

Times 9

Multiply. Then circle the answers in the maze. To get
through the maze, draw a line from one answer to the
next in the order you wrote them.

1. $\begin{array}{r} 3 \\ \times\,9 \\ \hline \end{array}$
2. $\begin{array}{r} 5 \\ \times\,9 \\ \hline \end{array}$
3. $\begin{array}{r} 9 \\ \times\,1 \\ \hline \end{array}$
4. $\begin{array}{r} 9 \\ \times\,2 \\ \hline \end{array}$
5. $\begin{array}{r} 9 \\ \times\,4 \\ \hline \end{array}$

6. $8 \times 9 =$ _____   **7.** $9 \times 6 =$ _____

8. $7 \times 9 =$ _____   **9.** $9 \times 9 =$ _____

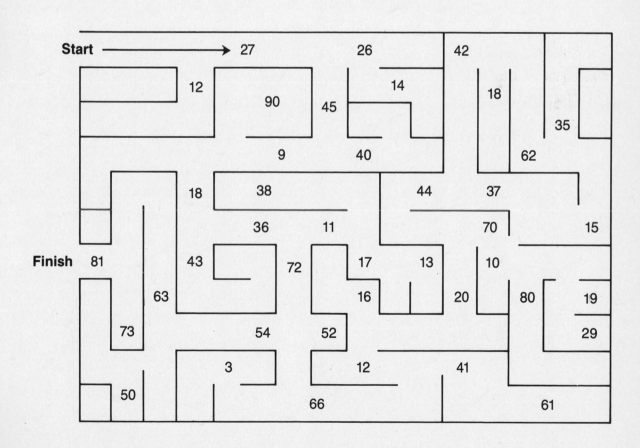

Addison-Wesley | All Rights Reserved

Jumbo Puzzle

Dear Family,
    Your child has been practicing multiplication facts. Complete the puzzle below together.

Trace and cut out the ten pieces. Match the factors and products.

Addison-Wesley | All Rights Reserved

Working Backward

Use the strategy Work Backward to solve each problem.
You may want to use a calculator.

1. Johnny had apples in a basket. His sister Mary ate 2 of them. He gave 8 away to his friends. Then he took 9 to school. He had 5 apples left. How many apples did he start with?

_____

2. June bought some stickers. She put 18 of them in one book. She put 10 in another. She gave 2 away. She had 6 stickers left. How many stickers did she buy?

_____

3. Joe had some trading cards. He lost 1. His friend gave him 3. He traded 10 for a ball. He had 9 left. How many cards did he have to start with?

_____

4. Larry had some peanuts. He ate 10. A friend gave him 9. Then he gave 4 away. He had 21 left. How many peanuts did he start with?

_____

5. Nina made string bracelets. She sold 10 at the school fair. She gave 10 to her friends. She made 5 more during the day. Then she had 10. How many bracelets did she start with?

_____

6. Write a problem of your own that can be solved using the strategy Work Backward.

_____

_____

_____

_____

_____

Addison-Wesley | All Rights Reserved

How Many Inside?

Each box has either 0, 1, or 2 balls inside. All the boxes with
the same letter have the same number of balls inside.

Ring the number of balls in each lettered box.

1. A + B B B = 1 ball

A	has	0	(1)	2 balls
B	has	(0)	1	2 balls

2. C C C + D D = 3 balls

C	has	0	1	2 balls
D	has	0	1	2 balls

3. E E E E + F F F F F F = 6 balls

E	has	0	1	2 balls
F	has	0	1	2 balls

4. G G G + H H = 7 balls

G	has	0	1	2 balls
H	has	0	1	2 balls

5. J J J + K K = 5 balls

J	has	0	1	2 balls
K	has	0	1	2 balls

6. L L L L + M M M = 8 balls

L	has	0	1	2 balls
M	has	0	1	2 balls

7. N N N + P = 2 balls

N	has	0	1	2 balls
P	has	0	1	2 balls

Addison-Wesley | All Rights Reserved

Name _____

Four in a Row

Dear Family,
   Your child has been practicing multiplication facts. Playing the game below will help reinforce the practice we are doing in school.

1. Make the number squares as shown at the bottom of the page.

2. Put them in a box or cup.

3. Gather about ten small markers for each player.

4. Each player chooses a game board.

5. Take turns drawing two numbers and multiplying. Both players place a marker on the product of the two numbers if it is shown on their game boards.

6. Return the numbers to the box or cup and mix.

7. The game ends when one player has four markers in a straight line in any direction (across, up and down, or diagonal).

Game Boards

6	20	48	18
32	12	56	15
27	35	72	10
45	54	24	40

12	56	16	8
54	18	21	30
48	36	27	24
28	42	14	63

Number Squares

2	3	4	5	6	7	8	9

Addison-Wesley | All Rights Reserved

Name _____

Number Riddles

Use the clues to solve the riddles.

1. One of my factors is 3. My digits add to 6. My other factor is not 5. What number am I?

_____

2. One of my factors is 4. My digits add to 3. What number am I?

_____

3. Our product is 18. We add to 11. What numbers are we?

_____

4. The sum of my digits is 3. One of my factors is 7. What number am I?

_____

5. I am 2 more than the product of 3 and 5. What number am I?

_____

6. I am 2 less than the product of 7 and 3. What number am I?

_____

7. Our product is 12. We add to 7. What numbers are we?

_____

8. Our product is 24. We add to 14. What numbers are we?

_____

9. My ones digit is twice my tens digit. One of my factors is 2 more than the other. The sum of my digits is 6. What number am I?

_____

10. One of my factors is 2 more than the other. My ones digit is 4 more than my tens digit. The sum of my digits is 6. What number am I?

_____

Addison-Wesley | All Rights Reserved

Name _____

Wanted Posters

The numbers on the posters are
wanted. Finish each poster
by writing a description of
the number. Identify each
number in at least two ways.
One of the ways should tell
about doubles. The first poster
has been completed for you.

```
WANTED

36

This number is
the sum of 20 + 16.
It is also the sum of
18 + 18.
```

1.
```
WANTED

32
```

2.
```
WANTED

30
```

3.
```
WANTED

38
```

4.
```
WANTED

28
```

Addison-Wesley | All Rights Reserved

Product Graphs

Color in the squares on the graphs to match each product.
The first three are done for you.

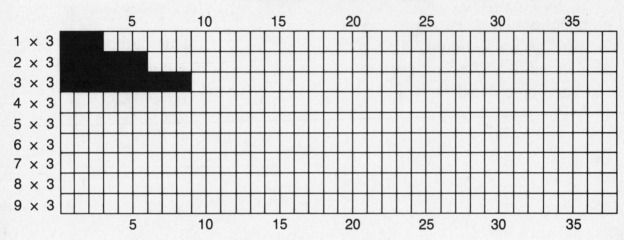

This graph is a stairstep pattern. Each new "step" is

_____ squares longer than the step above.

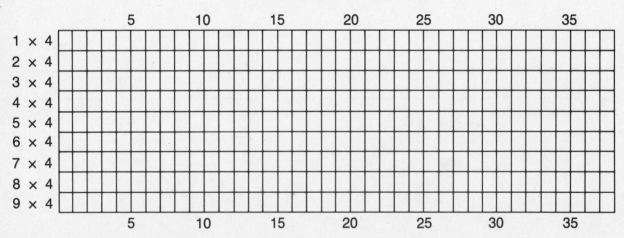

This stairstep pattern gets _____ squares longer each time. Describe what
the stairstep pattern for products of 5 will look like.

Addison-Wesley | All Rights Reserved

Name

Square Facts

Dear Family,
    Your child has learned to find fact products when each factor is the same. Here is an activity you can do together to practice the skill.

Write the equations for the dots below. Use multiplication.

1.

$5 \times 5 = 25$

2.

3.

4.

Write your own equations for squares. Then draw the dots to show each square fact.

5. _____ × _____ = _____   **6.** _____ × _____ = _____

Addison-Wesley | All Rights Reserved

Name _____

Take Two Steps

To walk well, watch your steps. You need to
watch your steps in math, too. Draw the steps
that you need to use to solve each multiple-step
problem. Then write the answer.

Choose from these steps.

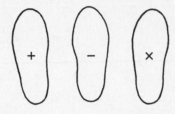

1. For the walk-a-thon, Donna
bought 5 rolls of crepe paper at
$2 each. She also bought a
paper bell for $6. How much
did the decorations cost?

step 1   step 2

_____

2. Troy printed 75 tickets and Fern
printed 80. They needed 150
tickets altogether. How many
extra tickets did they have?

step 1   step 2

_____

3. Jason helped set up 10 benches.
Each bench could seat 5 people.
Chun set up 30 folding chairs.
How many seats were there for
people to sit on?

step 1   step 2

_____

4. Vito bought 7 packs of paper
cups. Each pack had 25 cups.
If 120 walkers used 1 cup each,
how many cups were left over?

step 1   step 2

_____

Addison-Wesley | All Rights Reserved

Tic-Tac-Toe Facts

Play this game in teams of 3 or 4 players.

Rules

1. Write the numbers 2 through 9 on a separate sheet of paper. Then cut them out to make number squares.

2. Put the number squares in a box or cup.

3. Gather about ten small markers for each team. Buttons or beans will do.

4. Each team chooses one of the game boards below.

5. Take turns drawing two numbers and multiplying. Both teams place a marker on the product of the two numbers if it is shown on their game boards.

6. Return the numbers to the box and mix.

7. The game ends when one team has four markers in a straight line across, up and down, or diagonally.

Game Board

6	20	48	18
32	12	56	15
27	35	72	10
45	54	24	40

Game Board

12	56	16	8
54	18	21	30
48	36	27	24
28	42	14	63

Addison-Wesley | All Rights Reserved

Larger Products

There are only ten basic-fact products greater than 40. They are written on the balloons at the right. How many basic facts can you write with these numbers as products?

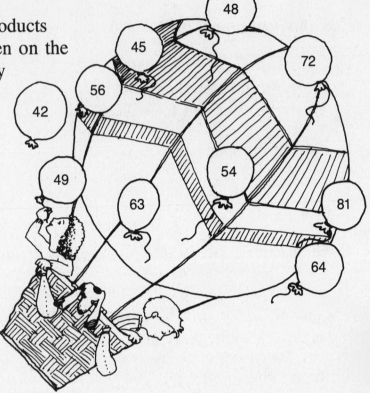

1. ___6___ × ___7___ = ___42___

2. ___7___ × ___6___ = ___42___

3. _____ × _____ = _____

4. _____ × _____ = _____

5. _____ × _____ = _____

6. _____ × _____ = _____

7. _____ × _____ = _____

8. _____ × _____ = _____

9. _____ × _____ = _____

10. _____ × _____ = _____

11. _____ × _____ = _____

12. _____ × _____ = _____

13. _____ × _____ = _____

14. _____ × _____ = _____

15. _____ × _____ = _____

16. _____ × _____ = _____

17. _____ × _____ = _____

Addison-Wesley | All Rights Reserved

Use with text page 250.

Name _____

Quick as a Bunny

First write the products as quickly as you can.
Check your answers. Draw a bunny in the hat
for each correct answer.

1. $6 \times 9 =$

54

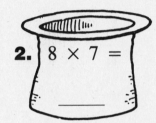

2. $8 \times 7 =$

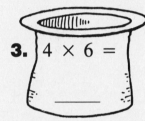

3. $4 \times 6 =$

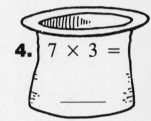

4. $7 \times 3 =$

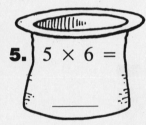

5. $5 \times 6 =$

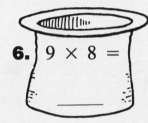

6. $9 \times 8 =$

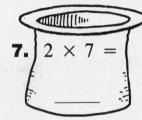

7. $2 \times 7 =$

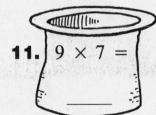

8. $9 \times 9 =$

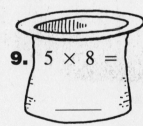

9. $5 \times 8 =$

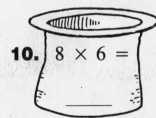

10. $8 \times 6 =$

11. $9 \times 7 =$

12. $7 \times 4 =$

13. $6 \times 7 =$

14. $2 \times 0 =$

15. $8 \times 8 =$

16. $7 \times 7 =$

Addison-Wesley | All Rights Reserved

Product Search

Use mental math to find the products. Write the answers
in the puzzle. The numbers across or down tell where
to begin writing the answers.

Across

1. $9 \times 1 \times 3$
2. $3 \times 6 \times 1$
5. $5 \times (3 \times 1)$
7. $(7 \times 2) \times 2$
8. $7 \times 1 \times 2$
11. $5 \times 2 \times 2$

Down

1. $(3 \times 4) \times 2$
3. $9 \times (3 \times 3)$
4. $4 \times 2 \times 4$
6. $2 \times (5 \times 5)$
9. $7 \times 3 \times 2$
10. $4 \times 2 \times 5$

Use with text pages 254–255.

Addison-Wesley | All Rights Reserved

Run the Race

Dear Family,
   This page will help your child find multiples. A multiple of a number is the product of that number and another factor. For example, 18 is a multiple of 1, 2, 3, 6, 9, and 18. You may want to participate by "entering the race."

To complete the race, identify and circle multiples of the number on each car. Stay on the right road for each car.

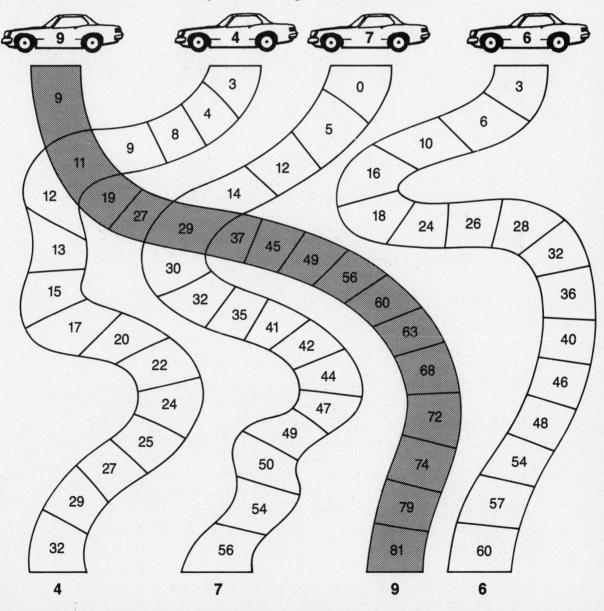

Addison-Wesley | All Rights Reserved

Package Patterns

A packing company uses this chart to decide how many items go into a box. There are six different box sizes. Work with two classmates to find the patterns and fill in the missing numbers.

	small (size 1)	medium (size 2)	large (size 3)	giant (size 4)	huge (size 5)	super huge (size 6)
erasers	6	12	18			
pencils	5	10	15			
pens	2		6	8		
rubber bands	7			28		
rulers				12	15	18
crayons					20	24
thumbtacks		16		32		48
glue		18	27			54

What is the pattern? Check with the other members of your group to write the patterns.

1. Eraser pattern: _____

2. Pencil pattern: _____

3. Pen pattern: _____

4. Rubber band pattern: _____

5. Ruler pattern: _____

6. Crayon pattern: _____

7. Thumbtack pattern: _____

8. Glue pattern: _____

Addison-Wesley | All Rights Reserved

More Number Riddles

Solve these number riddles. Each riddle has more than
one solution.

1.
My ones digit is twice my
tens digit. One of my factors
is 3.

What number am I?

_____

2.
My digits add to 9. One of
my factors is 6.

What number am I?

_____

3.
My digits add to 6. One of
my factors is 3.

What number am I?

_____

4.
One of my factors is one
more than the other. I am
a number less than 30.

What number am I?

_____

5.
I am a number greater than
20. The sum of my factors
is 11.

What number am I?

_____

6.
I am a multiple of 2, 3, 4,
and 6. I am greater than 10
but less than 30.

What number am I?

_____

Addison-Wesley | All Rights Reserved

Name _____

Figure It Out

Solve each riddle. Write the name of the space figure.
Then draw an object that is an example of the figure.

sphere	cube	cone	rectangular prism	pyramid	cylinder

1. I have no corners. I will roll. I am round like a ball. What am I?

2. 4 of my faces are triangles that come together in a point at the top. What am I?

_____

_____

3. I have only 1 flat face. I can roll. I have no straight edges. What am I?

4. I have only flat faces. They are all the same size. What am I?

_____

_____

5. I can have 3 pairs of different-size rectangular faces. They are all flat. What am I?

6. I have 2 flat faces. I can roll. What am I?

_____

_____

Addison-Wesley | All Rights Reserved

Making Boxes

You can fold this figure to make an open
box with the black square on the bottom:

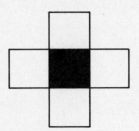 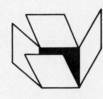

Each figure below can be folded to make an open box.
Color the square that will be on the bottom.

Trace, cut, and fold the boxes to check your answers.

1.

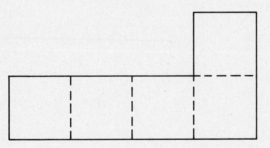

2.

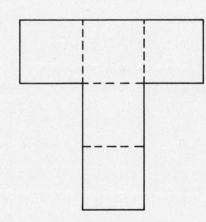

3.

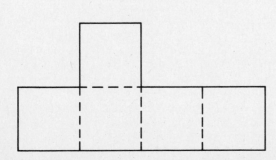

4.

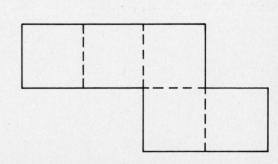

Addison-Wesley | All Rights Reserved

Point to Point

Draw a polygon that matches each description. Remember
that polygons are closed plane figures with segments
that join at points.

1. A small rectangle

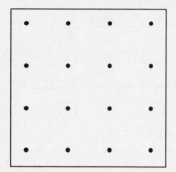

2. A triangle with 2 equal sides

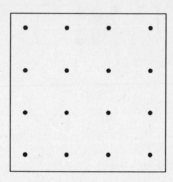

3. A small square

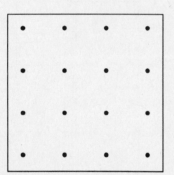

4. A triangle with 3 different
length sides

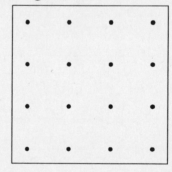

5. A large rectangle

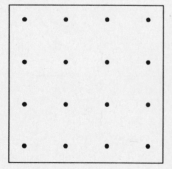

6. A large square

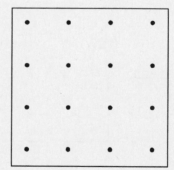

Addison-Wesley | All Rights Reserved

Drawing Angles

On each piece of dot paper, draw the polygon described.

1. a triangle with 1 right angle

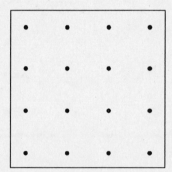

2. a 4-sided polygon with exactly 2 right angles

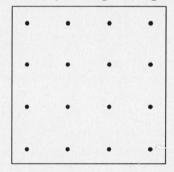

3. a 4-sided polygon with 4 different angles

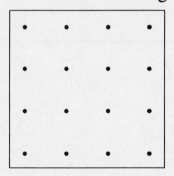

4. a triangle with 1 angle greater than a right angle

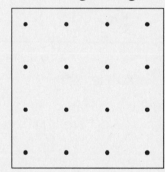

5. a 4-sided polygon with 2 angles greater than a right angle

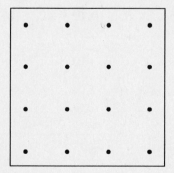

6. a triangle with 3 angles less than a right angle

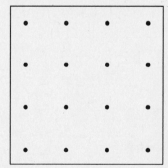

Addison-Wesley | All Rights Reserved

Name _____

In Between

You can check an answer by finding two estimates. Find the first estimate by rounding down to the nearest 10¢ and the second by rounding up to the nearest 10¢. The answer should come between the two estimates.

Complete these problems by finding two estimates and the actual total. Ring the closer estimate.

1. Mary estimated that 3 hot pads

would cost between

($2.40) and $2.70 .

The actual total is $2.46 .

Which estimate is closer?

2. Tony estimated that 3 bookmarks

and a hot pad would cost

between _____, and _____.

The actual total is _____.

Which estimate is closer?

3. Krista estimated that a bookmark

and a key chain would cost

between _____ and _____.

The actual total is _____.

Which estimate is closer?

4. Peggy estimated that 4 key chains

and 3 can openers would cost

between **$3.70** and _____.

The actual total is _____.

Which estimate is closer?

Addison-Wesley | All Rights Reserved

Tangram Puzzle

Dear Family,
   Your child has been comparing polygons according to sides and angles.
Here is an activity you can do together.

Trace and cut out the seven pieces of the tangram.

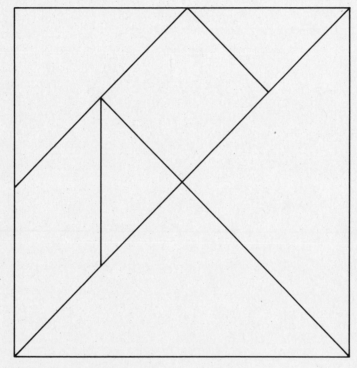

Use all seven pieces to make these pictures.

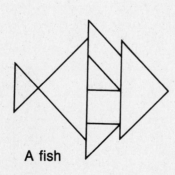

A fish

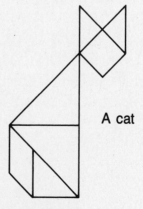

A cat

What other pictures can you make with all seven pieces?

Addison-Wesley | All Rights Reserved

Name _____

Two Parts of the Picture

Finish each picture by drawing the missing part. Then draw
a line of symmetry on the completed picture.

1.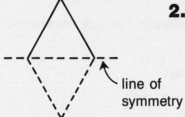

line of
symmetry

diamond

2.

heart

3.

butterfly

4.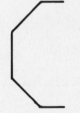

stop sign

5.

cat

6.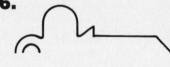

key

7.

starfish

8.

moose

9.

lamp

Addison-Wesley | All Rights Reserved

The Tangram Pieces

Dear Family,
   Our math class has been studying geometry. Many new terms have been introduced. If two figures are the same size and shape, we call them "congruent." The exercises below give your child an opportunity to work with you on some congruence puzzles.

Here are seven tangram pieces. Trace and cut out a copy of each piece. Then use your pieces to answer the questions below.

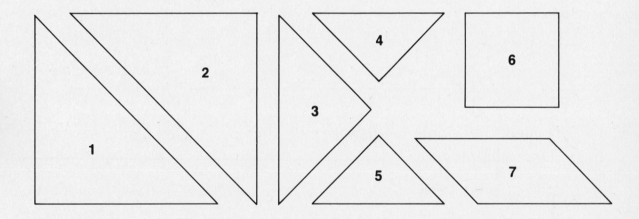

1. Pieces 1 and 2 are congruent. They match in both size and shape. Which other two pieces are congruent?

_____

2. Which of the following pairs of pieces do not match in shape or size? Ring them.

6 and 4   1 and 5   2 and 3   2 and 6

3. There are two ways to make a triangle that is congruent to triangle 1. Each uses three pieces. List the pieces for each way.

_____   _____

Addison-Wesley | All Rights Reserved

Line Puzzle

Trace the shape below and cut out its 6 pieces.

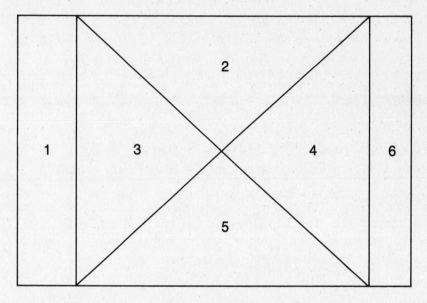

1. Place 2 pieces at a time to show parallel lines and intersecting lines. Draw the pieces.

parallel lines   intersecting lines

2. Draw other pieces you can use to show parallel lines or intersecting lines.

Addison-Wesley | All Rights Reserved

Point Game

Play the Point Game in 2 teams: Team X and Team Y.
Each team has 3 players.

Rules:

1. Each team writes on a separate sheet of paper
   a number pair for a point on the graph below.
2. Teams take turns asking two questions about
   the location of a point on the graph.
   Example: Is it 2 units to the right? Is it up 5 units?
3. When a team correctly guesses a number pair,
   a member from that team marks the location on the graph
   with an X or a Y.
4. The first team to make 10 correct guesses wins.

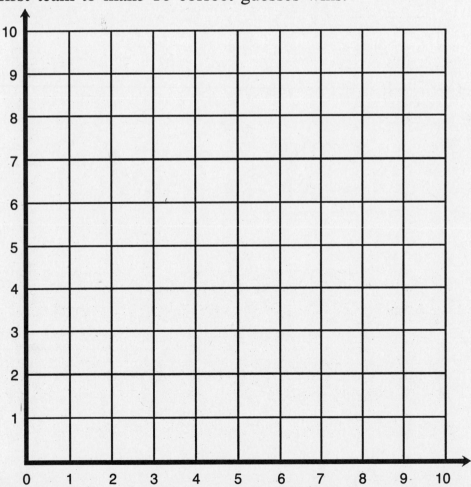

Addison-Wesley | All Rights Reserved

Name _____

Blooming Baskets

Dear Family,
   Our class is learning division. Observe while your child works through this page. Providing similar opportunities to make equal groups will strengthen your child's understanding of division.

Draw baskets under the flowers to make equal groups.

1.   2 baskets

$$10 \div 2 = \underline{5}$$

2.   5 baskets

$$20 \div 5 = \underline{\hphantom{5}}$$

3.   4 baskets

$$16 \div 4 = \underline{\hphantom{5}}$$

4.   3 baskets

$$9 \div 3 = \underline{\hphantom{5}}$$

5.   4 baskets

$$8 \div 4 = \underline{\hphantom{5}}$$

6.   3 baskets

$$18 \div 3 = \underline{\hphantom{5}}$$

Addison-Wesley | All Rights Reserved

Name _____

Find the Ways

Use counters. Find ways you can share the total
number equally. Complete each chart.

Total Number of Marbles	Number of Marbles in Each Bag	Number of Bags	Division Equation
12			
12			
12			
12			

Total Number of Buttons	Number of Buttons on Each Shirt	Number of Shirts	Division Equation
24			
24			
24			
24			
24			
24			

Compare your equations with a partner.
Are they the same?

Addison-Wesley | All Rights Reserved

Name _____

Equal Beagle

The Equal Beagle always wants groups to be equal in number.
Look at the bones below. Equal Beagle moved some of the
bones to make the groups equal.

Before Equal Beagle   After Equal Beagle

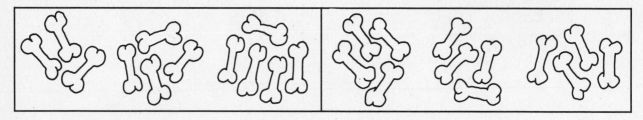

Redraw each group below to show what Equal Beagle would do.

Before Equal Beagle   After Equal Beagle

Addison-Wesley | All Rights Reserved

Name _____

Boxes and Division

Dear Family,
   Our class has just learned about dividing by 4. Observe as your child completes this page. You may wish to help your child work out the problems with small objects.

The Box-em Machine puts the same number of items in each box.

Complete this record sheet for the machine and solve the equations.

Record for the Box-em Machine				
Item	Input (Number of Items)	Number in Each Box	Output (Number of Boxes)	Equation
crayons	16	4	4	$16 \div 4 = 4$
pens	12	4		
toy cars	28	4		
marbles	24	4		
rulers	16	4		
table-tennis balls	32	4		
books	20	4		

Addison-Wesley | All Rights Reserved

Who Visits Dinosaurs?

Analyze the bar graph. Then write your own questions using data from the graph. Write at least three questions. Give them to a classmate to answer.

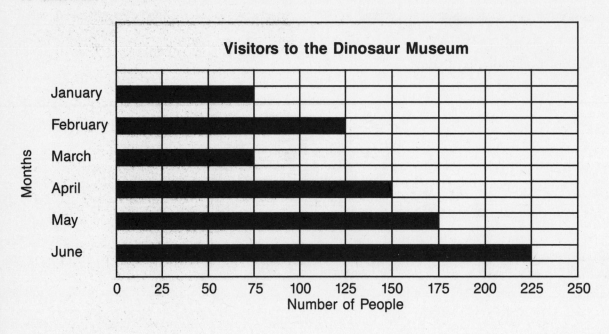

Visitors to the Dinosaur Museum

Months / Number of People

_____

_____

_____

_____

_____

_____

_____

Addison-Wesley | All Rights Reserved

Design by Division

Discover the design. Work with a classmate. Color the
numbers in the grid that can be divided evenly by
3, 4, and 5. Follow the code to color the squares.

Code:
Can be divided by 3 → yellow
Can be divided by 4 → green
Can be divided by 5 → blue

10	2	38	13	22	1	27
23	50	7	41	19	35	34
11	29	9	28	18	49	7
19	34	16	32	8	43	26
17	2	3	4	6	13	31
47	5	26	37	7	25	46
21	53	23	11	59	14	5

Work with your partner to create a grid design of your own using
numbers that can be divided evenly by 3, 4, and 5.

Addison-Wesley | All Rights Reserved

Name _____

Trumpets and Trombones

Solve.

1. Jody practices the drums 4 days a week. She practices 2 hours each day. How many hours does she practice a week?

   _____

2. There are 36 students in the school band. They march in rows of 4. How many rows are there?

   _____

3. Jody can choose what she wants to do in the band. She can play the triangle, snare drums, or bass drum. She can march in the front or the back. How many choices does she have?

   _____

4. The brass section has 4 bugles, 5 trombones, and 2 tubas. There are twice as many trumpets as trombones. How many horns are in the brass section?

   _____

5. The band hoped to play 6 outdoor concerts. Each concert would be 45 minutes long. Because of rain, 2 concerts were not played. How many hours of outdoor concert time did the band play?

   _____

6. The evening meal at the band festival cost each student $1.25. The band members could buy extra food in addition to the $1.25 meal. Extra milk was 15¢ a carton and an extra sandwich was 75¢. Jody spent $2.30 for her meal. What did she eat?

   _____

   _____

   _____

Addison-Wesley | All Rights Reserved

Name _____

Multiplication and Division Are Related

Solve the problem. Then complete the fact family. **Order of answers may vary.**

1. $2 \times 4 =$ _____   _____   _____   _____

2. _____ $6 \times 4 =$ _____   _____   _____

3. _____   _____   _____ $6 \div 2 =$ _____

4. _____ $5 \times 3 =$ _____   _____   _____

5. _____   _____ $12 \div 4 =$ _____   _____

6. $4 \times 7 =$ _____   _____   _____   _____

7. _____   _____   _____ $10 \div 2 =$ _____

8. _____   _____ $8 \div 2 =$ _____   _____

9. $8 \times 5 =$ _____   _____   _____   _____

Write your own problems. Write a fact family for
each set of factors and products you use.

10. _____   _____   _____   _____

11. _____   _____   _____   _____

Addison-Wesley | All Rights Reserved

Division Relationship

Write and solve a division equation for each
multiplication equation.

1. $1 \times \boxed{} = 9$ $\quad\quad \underline{9} \div \underline{1} = \underline{9}$

2. $7 \times \boxed{} = 21$ $\quad\quad \underline{} \div \underline{} = \underline{}$

3. $15 \times \boxed{} = 15$ $\quad\quad \underline{} \div \underline{} = \underline{}$

4. $12 \times \boxed{} = 0$ $\quad\quad \underline{} \div \underline{} = \underline{}$

5. $3 \times \boxed{} = 18$ $\quad\quad \underline{} \div \underline{} = \underline{}$

Write $\times$ or $\div$ for each $\bigcirc$.

6. $7 \bigcirc 2 = 14$ $\quad\quad\quad\quad$ **7.** $14 \bigcirc 2 = 7$

8. $8 \bigcirc 4 = 2$ $\quad\quad\quad\quad$ **9.** $0 \bigcirc 2 = 0$

10. $2 \bigcirc 6 = 12$ $\quad\quad\quad$ **11.** $3 \bigcirc 3 = 9$

12. $2 \bigcirc 9 = 18$ $\quad\quad\quad$ **13.** $8 \bigcirc 1 = 8$

14. $25 \bigcirc 1 = 25$ $\quad\quad\quad$ **15.** $5 \bigcirc 1 = 5$

Addison-Wesley | All Rights Reserved

Write Your Own Problems

Write 2 division problems showing different actions. Use the data in the picture.

Fred's magazine stand looks like this:

1. **Action**: Share a set equally.

_____

_____

_____

_____

equation: _____ ÷ _____ = _____

2. **Action**: Take away same-size sets repeatedly.

_____

_____

_____

_____

equation: _____ ÷ _____ = _____

3. Draw a picture of your own showing data for a division problem. Then write a division problem.

_____

_____

_____

_____

_____

equation: _____ ÷ _____ = _____

Addison-Wesley | All Rights Reserved

Name _____

Rafting Problems

Tom and Becky made these rafts. They had a few problems.
Parts of the rafts have sunk below the water.

Figure out how many white boards they used in each raft.
Then write a division equation that shows how you know.

1.

(18 nails in all)

White boards: _3_

18÷6=3

2.

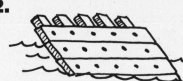

(20 nails in all)

White boards: ____

_____

3.

(24 nails in all)

White boards: ____

_____

4.

(28 nails in all)

White boards: ____

_____

5.

(24 nails in all)

White boards: ____

_____

6.

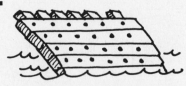

(30 nails in all)

White boards: ____

_____

Addison-Wesley | All Rights Reserved

Name _____

Find the Price

Solve these problems. First fill in how much one item costs. Then fill in the other blanks.

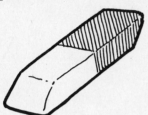

1.

7 for 63¢

1 for _____   2 for _____

3 for _____   4 for _____

2.

6 for 54¢

1 for _____   7 for _____

4 for _____   5 for _____

3.

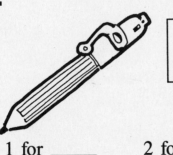

·STICKERS·

7 for 49¢

1 for _____   2 for _____

3 for _____   4 for _____

4.

6 for 42¢

1 for _____   6 for _____

5 for _____   8 for _____

5.

6 for 48¢

1 for _____   2 for _____

4 for _____   5 for _____

6.

7 for 56¢

1 for _____   3 for _____

6 for _____   7 for _____

Addison-Wesley | All Rights Reserved

Write a Related Problem

Work in small groups to solve the problems below and write a related problem that can be solved using the same strategy. Exchange your problems with another group and solve each other's problems.

Related Problems

1. In the bus line, Jill stood between Roy and Carmen. Carmen was in front of Jill. Wan was after Roy. Who were first and last in line?

_____

_____

_____

Strategy: _____

_____

Answer: _____

_____

2. Frank can have his birthday party either Saturday or Sunday. He can have it at the roller rink or at the ice-skating rink. How many choices does Frank have?

_____

_____

_____

Strategy: _____

_____

Answer: _____

_____

3. At the fair, 3 classes of 9 students each collected money for their school. How many students in all collected money?

_____

_____

_____

Strategy: _____

_____

Answer: _____

_____

Addison-Wesley | All Rights Reserved

Forgetful George

George and Celia need to bring a total of 6 colored pencils to school. They used the chart below to decide how many pencils each should bring. The top of the chart shows how many Celia needs to bring if George forgets and brings none at all.

1. Find the other combinations and complete the chart.

2. Make a point on the graph for each number pair on the chart. Then connect the points.

George	Celia
0	6

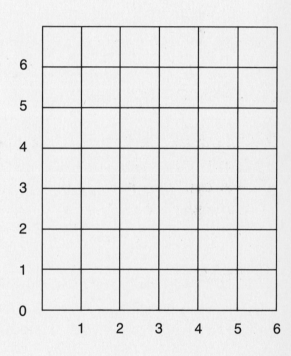

3. What do you notice when you connect the points?

_____

Addison-Wesley | All Rights Reserved

Dotty Equations

How many different equations can you write about the dots below?
Draw lines in each picture to show your thinking. Use × or ÷.

Examples:

$$4 \times 6 = 24$$

$$24 \div 3 = 8$$

1.

_____

_____

2.

_____

_____

3.

_____

_____

4.

_____

_____

5.

_____

_____

6.

_____

_____

Addison-Wesley | All Rights Reserved

Name _____

Nifty Nines

Dear Family,
   Your child has been learning division facts that involve dividing by 9. Here is an activity you can do together.

Nine is an unusual number. Some interesting things happen when you multiply or divide by it.

1. Divide: $18 \div 9 =$ _____ $54 \div 9 =$ _____ $63 \div 9 =$ _____

$81 \div 9 =$ _____ $36 \div 9 =$ _____ $45 \div 9 =$ _____

$27 \div 9 =$ _____ $72 \div 9 =$ _____

2. Add the digits of the first number in each of the problems above. What is the sum each time? _____

3. In each problem above, subtract the tens digit in the first number from the quotient. What is the difference each time? _____

4. Multiply:

$$\begin{array}{cccc} 4 & \quad 9 & \quad 6 & \quad 8 \\ \times 9 & \quad \times 9 & \quad \times 9 & \quad \times 9 \\ \hline \end{array}$$

5. Add the digits of each product. What number do you get each time? _____

Addison-Wesley | All Rights Reserved

Around the World

Dear Family,
Your child has been practicing division facts. You may wish to play the game below with your child to help reinforce our work in math class.

1. Each player chooses a small marker.

2. Each player chooses a track and places a marker on **Start**.

3. Take turns. Find the answer to the problem where the marker is and then move the marker ahead that number of spaces.

4. The first player to reach **Finish** wins.

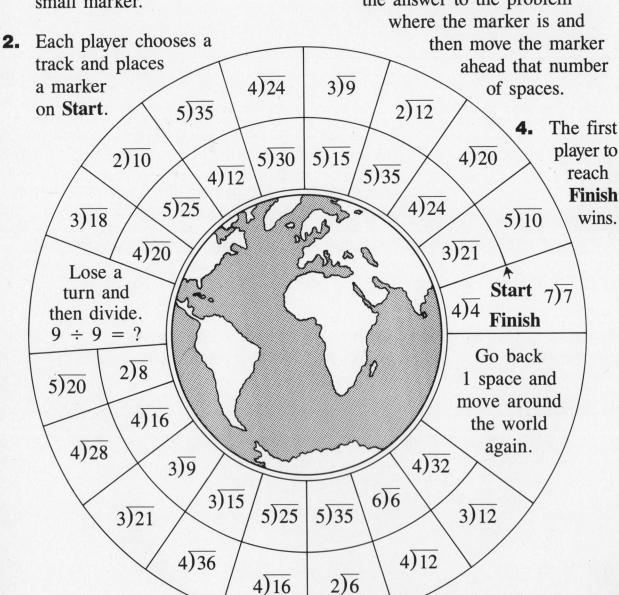

Addison-Wesley | All Rights Reserved

Star Trackers

A. 4×5 _____   **G.** 8×7 _____   **M.** 8×1 _____

B. 9×1 _____   **H.** 6×8 _____   **N.** 2×6 _____

C. 6×3 _____   **I.** 2×4 _____   **O.** 3×3 _____

D. 2×7 _____   **J.** 5×2 _____   **P.** 4×6 _____

E. 8×5 _____   **K.** 4×9 _____   **Q.** 7×3 _____

F. 9×8 _____   **L.** 3×4 _____   **R.** 1×6 _____

Compare answers with your classmates. Look for one answer
that appears in all 3 columns. Match the letters for that answer
to the letters below. Ring the names of the players.

A. Pat   **E.** Dan   **I.** Ray   **M.** Mia   **Q.** Guy

B. Ida   **F.** Liz   **J.** Ali   **N.** Ben   **R.** Kay

C. Tod   **G.** Joy   **K.** Van   **O.** Ann

D. Kim   **H.** Eve   **L.** Vic   **P.** Ned

Addison-Wesley | All Rights Reserved

Name _____

Product Wheels

Dear Family,
   Your child has been learning to multiply 1-digit numbers by multiples of 10. The exercises below give your child an opportunity to share this skill with you.

A product is given in the center of each wheel. Put two numbers on each spoke so that their product is the center number.

1.

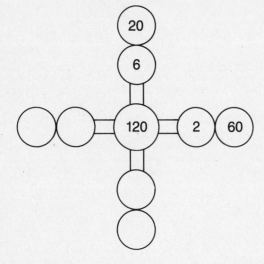

2.

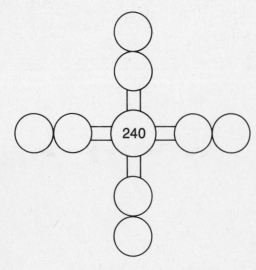

3.

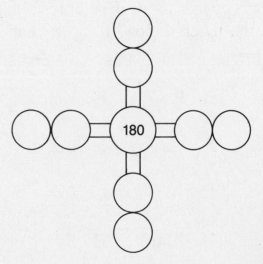

Addison-Wesley | All Rights Reserved

School Time Show your answers

~~Estimate each product by rounding the 2-digit numbers to the nearest 10. Then tell whether the exact answer is over or under your estimate.~~

1. Every week he is in school, Danny attends 2 hours of science classes on each of 4 days. If he is in school for 38 weeks, about how many hours of science classes will Danny attend?

_____

2. Every week she is in school, Barbara does about 4 hours of math homework and 5 hours of language arts homework. If she is in school for 34 weeks this year, about how many hours will she spend on math and language arts homework?

_____

3. Joyce's after-school dance class met 3 days each week, for 2 hours each day, for 36 weeks. She missed 5 weeks of classes. About how How many hours of dance class did she attend?

_____

4. Mr. Leary teaches 2 movement classes, 3 dance classes, and 4 gymnastics classes each week. If school is in session for 39 weeks, about how many classes does he teach altogether?

_____

Addison-Wesley | All Rights Reserved

Ring the Exercise

Follow the instructions to complete the following.

1. Ring the exercise in which you will not need to trade.

4×16 5×1 6×13

2. Ring the exercise in which you will need to trade.

4×12 3×23 5×14

3. Ring the two exercises that will have the same product.

5×18 6×17 18×5

4. Ring the exercise with the greatest product.

4×32 4×33 5×32

5. Ring the exercise with the smallest product.

5×29 4×29 5×28

6. Ring the exercise whose product is greater than one of the products but smaller than the other.

3×14 4×13 3×13

7. Ring the exercise with the greatest product. Then write an exercise with a product that is greater by 30.

2×15 3×15 4×15

Addison-Wesley | All Rights Reserved

Name _____

Balancing Act

Find the products. For each problem you need to trade, draw an apple on the left side of the scale. For each problem you can solve without trading, draw an apple on the right side.

1. $\begin{array}{r} 12 \\ \times\ 3 \\ \hline \end{array}$
2. $\begin{array}{r} 13 \\ \times\ 6 \\ \hline \end{array}$
3. $\begin{array}{r} 23 \\ \times\ 4 \\ \hline \end{array}$
4. $\begin{array}{r} 32 \\ \times\ 2 \\ \hline \end{array}$
5. $\begin{array}{r} 18 \\ \times\ 5 \\ \hline \end{array}$

6. $\begin{array}{r} 25 \\ \times\ 3 \\ \hline \end{array}$
7. $\begin{array}{r} 41 \\ \times\ 2 \\ \hline \end{array}$
8. $\begin{array}{r} 33 \\ \times\ 3 \\ \hline \end{array}$
9. $\begin{array}{r} 19 \\ \times\ 5 \\ \hline \end{array}$
10. $\begin{array}{r} 27 \\ \times\ 3 \\ \hline \end{array}$

11. $\begin{array}{r} 11 \\ \times\ 7 \\ \hline \end{array}$
12. $\begin{array}{r} 21 \\ \times\ 4 \\ \hline \end{array}$
13. $\begin{array}{r} 16 \\ \times\ 4 \\ \hline \end{array}$
14. $\begin{array}{r} 28 \\ \times\ 2 \\ \hline \end{array}$
15. $\begin{array}{r} 12 \\ \times\ 2 \\ \hline \end{array}$

Addison-Wesley | All Rights Reserved

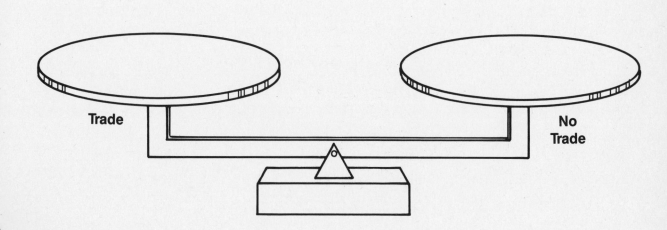

Trade

No Trade

Which way will the scale tip? _____

Name _____

Missing Digits

Dear Family,
   Work with your child to find the missing digits in the first three examples below. Then you and your child may enjoy making up some multiplication exercises that will result in the products given.

Find the missing digits.

1.
```
   2 [ ]
 ×   5
 ―――――
[ ] 2 0
```

2.
```
 [ ] [ ]
 ×   3
 ―――――
 2 4 9
```

3.
```
 [ ] [ ]
 ×   5
 ―――――
 1 7 0
```

Make your own multiplication exercises with these products.

4.
```
 [ ] [ ]
 ×  [ ]
 ―――――
   7 8
```

5.
```
 [ ] [ ]
 ×  [ ]
 ―――――
   6 8
```

6.
```
 [ ] [ ]
 ×  [ ]
 ―――――
 1 6 8
```

7.
```
 [ ] [ ]
 ×  [ ]
 ―――――
 1 9 2
```

8.
```
 [ ] [ ]
 ×  [ ]
 ―――――
 1 8 4
```

9.
```
 [ ] [ ]
 ×  [ ]
 ―――――
 2 2 8
```

10.
```
 [ ] [ ]
 ×  [ ]
 ―――――
 2 2 4
```

11.
```
 [ ] [ ]
 ×  [ ]
 ―――――
 1 5 6
```

12.
```
 [ ] [ ]
 ×  [ ]
 ―――――
 3 8 8
```

Addison-Wesley | All Rights Reserved

Missing Digits

Find the missing digits.

1.
```
    5 □
  ×   4
  ─────
  2 2 4
```

2.
```
    □ 8
  ×   2
  ─────
  1 5 6
```

3.
```
    4 3
  ×   □
  ─────
  1 7 2
```

4.
```
    6 7
  ×   3
  ─────
  □ □ 1
```

5.
```
    2 □
  ×   5
  ─────
  □ 2 0
```

6.
```
    □ □
  ×   3
  ─────
  2 4 9
```

7.
```
    □ □
  ×   5
  ─────
  1 7 0
```

8.
```
    □ 4
  ×   4
  ─────
  2 1 □
```

Create your own multiplication exercises with these products.

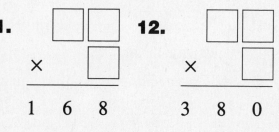

9.
```
    □ □
  ×   □
  ─────
    7 8
```

10.
```
    □ □
  ×   □
  ─────
    6 8
```

11.
```
    □ □
  ×   □
  ─────
  1 6 8
```

12.
```
    □ □
  ×   □
  ─────
  3 8 0
```

13.
```
    □ □
  ×   □
  ─────
  1 9 2
```

14.
```
    □ □
  ×   □
  ─────
  1 8 4
```

15.
```
    □ □
  ×   □
  ─────
  2 2 8
```

16.
```
    □ □
  ×   □
  ─────
  3 8 8
```

Addison-Wesley | All Rights Reserved

Name _____

Use a Calculation Method

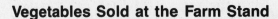

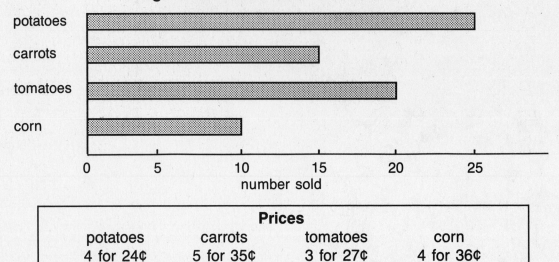

Vegetables Sold at the Farm Stand

number sold

Prices			
potatoes	carrots	tomatoes	corn
4 for 24¢	5 for 35¢	3 for 27¢	4 for 36¢

Write 2 problems that you can solve with mental math. Use the data above.

1. _____

_____

_____

Answer: _____

2. _____

_____

_____

Answer: _____

Write 2 problems that you can solve with pencil and paper or a calculator. Use the data above.

3. _____

_____

_____

Answer: _____

4. _____

_____

_____

Answer: _____

Addison-Wesley | All Rights Reserved

Name _____

At the Fruit Stand

Work with a partner. You will need a number
cube and play money.
- Take turns choosing a fruit to buy.
- Roll the number cube to see how many
  pounds of that fruit you will buy.
- Estimate the total cost.
- Multiply to find the actual cost.

🍒 Fruit Stand 🍇	
apples	$ 0.51/pound
pears	$ 0.45/pound
oranges	$ 0.62/pound
grapes	$ 0.79/pound
peaches	$ 0.86/pound
bananas	$ 0.38/pound

Give your partner more than enough money to pay for
the fruit. Your partner counts up to give you change.
Take turns being the shopper and the fruit stand owner.
Record what you do on the chart.

Fruit	Number of Pounds	Cost for Each Pound	Estimated Total Cost	Actual Total Cost

Addison-Wesley | All Rights Reserved

Calculator Tic-Tac-Toe

Play with a friend. You will need a calculator.

1. Take turns. Choose two different numbers from the multiplication box and find the product.
2. Subtract 10 from the product.
3. Add 25 to the difference.
4. Find the sum on the game board and place an **X** or **O** on it. (If the sum has already been marked, play passes to the other player.)
5. The first player to mark three numbers in a row horizontally, vertically, or diagonally is the winner.

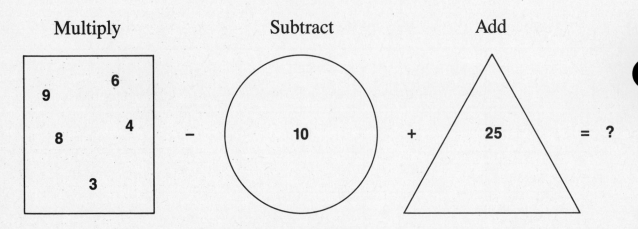

Multiply Subtract Add

Game Board

69	39	63
42	87	33
47	27	51

Addison-Wesley | All Rights Reserved

Name _____

Measuring Paths

Use a centimeter ruler to find the length of each path.

1. _____ cm

2. _____ cm

One 12-centimeter path is shown on the graph paper. The end points are marked with dots. Work with a partner to plan and draw other 12-centimeter paths on the graph paper. Mark each end point with a dot. Stay on the lines.

Addison-Wesley | All Rights Reserved

Matching Measures

Write three items for each measurement.
Then compare your answers with a classmate's.

1. about 2 decimeters

_____

_____

_____

2. about 1 meter

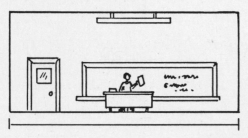

_____

_____

_____

3. about 5 meters

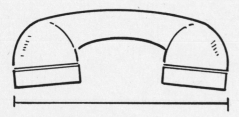

_____

_____

_____

4. about 1 kilometer

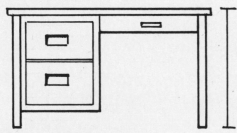

_____

_____

_____

Addison-Wesley | All Rights Reserved

Name _____

Hidden Squares

Find the area of each shaded rectangle in square units.
Be sure to count the parts you cannot see.

Addison-Wesley | All Rights Reserved

Name _____

Hidden Cubes

Dear Family,
   Your child has been learning about the number of units that fills a geometric space, or volume. You may enjoy working with your child to find the volume of each figure below.

Count the number of cubic units in each figure. Remember to count the cubic units you cannot see. Then write the volume of each figure in cubic units.

1.

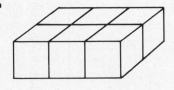

_____

2.

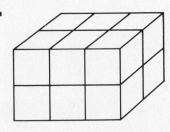

_____

3.

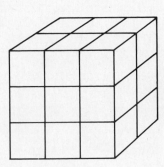

_____

4.

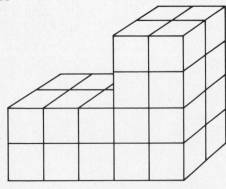

_____

5.

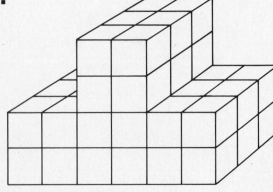

_____

Addison-Wesley | All Rights Reserved

Addison-Wesley | All Rights Reserved

Who Is Cool?

Write the letter of the thermometer showing the temperature that matches each description.

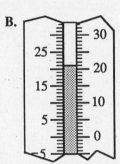

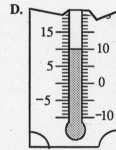
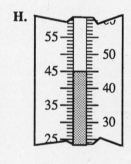

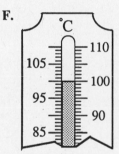
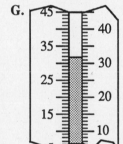

1. The temperature in your freezer _____

2. The temperature of boiling water _____

3. The temperature on a hot summer day _____

4. The temperature of a glass of ice water _____

5. The temperature of hot soup _____

6. The temperature on a day that is just right for running _____

7. The temperature on a day your snowman will not melt _____

8. The hottest temperature to register on the thermometer _____

Name _____

A Metric Measures Maze

Each box in the maze shows a metric
measurement of capacity or length. Only
eight of the boxes contain sensible measures.

Make your way through the maze from **Start**
to **Finish** by finding a path of sensible
measures. You can move sideways ↔ ,
diagonally ↗ ↘ , and up and down ↕ .

Start

A punch bowl holds 3 L.	A coffee cup holds 1 L.	A pencil is 50 cm long.	Ralph is 2 km tall.
The museum is 12 km away.	Your shoe is 4 cm long.	A bathtub can hold 30 L of water.	France is 5,000 m away from Canada.
Your dog is 20 m high.	A ladder is 5 m long.	A glass can hold 2,000 mL of water.	Your smile is 6 cm wide.
A toad can jump 10 m.	Lucy drinks 50 L of water in a week.	A goldfish swims 10 cm each day.	A cup might hold 75 mL of juice.
The distance from Boston to San Diego is about 6,000 dm.	Your toe is 25 cm long.	Pat hiked 5 km.	A car's gas tank holds 200 L of gas.
A bucket holds 100 mL of water.	A sunflower might grow to a height of 2 km.	A baseball bat is 5 L long.	A cereal bowl holds 250 mL of milk.

Finish

Addison-Wesley | All Rights Reserved

Metric Olympics

How do your skills at estimating weights measure up?
Enter the Metric Measurement Olympics to find out!
Work in small groups.

First Event: 1-Kilogram Weigh

Object: To estimate a total weight of 1 kg.

Gather assorted objects from around the
classroom. Place them in a bag. Fill your
bag until you estimate that it weighs about
1 kilogram.

Select one group member to weigh each bag.
The winner is the student whose bag weighs
closest to 1 kilogram.

Repeat the event, each time filling your bag
with different objects. Record your results.
See if your estimates get closer to 1 kilogram.

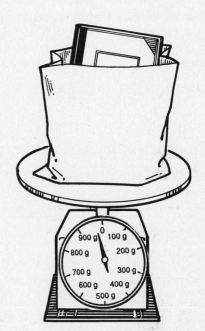

Second Event: 100-Gram Weigh

Object: To estimate a total weight of 100 g.

Follow the steps for the 1-kg weigh. This
time the winner is the student with the bag
that weighs closest to 100 grams.

Repeat the event and keep track of your
results. See if your estimates get closer
to 100 grams.

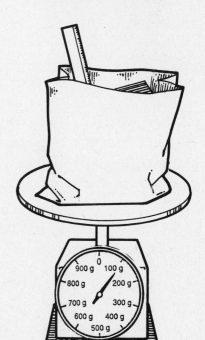

Addison-Wesley | All Rights Reserved

Name _____

Measure for Measure

Dear Family,
   Your child is learning to decide whether an actual measurement is needed or whether an estimate is sufficient when solving problems. Here is an activity you can do with your child.

Decide whether to estimate or to give an exact measurement in each situation. Then write **exact** or **estimated** on the blank.

1. Lee wants to follow the recipe to make fruit punch. He needs to know how much of each kind of juice to use.

Use _____
measurements for this recipe.

Use 3 cups of orange juice.
Use 1 cup of grapefruit juice.
Stir and pour.

2. Sandy wants to find the buried treasure. She needs to follow the directions to find the treasure.

Use _____
measurements.

Find the distance between the 2 rocks. You will find the treasure exactly halfway between these rocks.

3. Wendy wants to cut a small wood board into 3 pieces to make different shapes.

Use _____
measurements.

Carve each piece of wood into a plane figure.

4. Troy's airplane model is 23 cm long. His model ship is 31 cm long. He needs to know which model to put in which box.

Use _____
measurements.

Pack each model in a separate box that fits.

Addison-Wesley | All Rights Reserved

At the Diner

You work at a diner. As food comes from the kitchen, your job is to cut it into equal serving pieces. Draw lines to show how you would divide each food so that it serves the number of people shown. Complete the sentence for each food.

1.

for 6 people

This rye bread is cut into

_____ .

2.

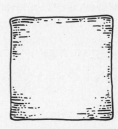

for 4 people

Each person will get a

_____ of a blueberry tart.

3.

for 10 people

I divided the whole wheat

bread into _____ .

4.

for 8 people

The French bread is cut into

_____ .

5.

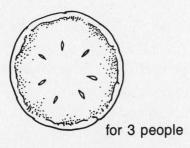

for 3 people

Each person can have a

_____ of the meat pie.

6.

for 5 people

A _____ of the carrot cake will serve one person.

Addison-Wesley | All Rights Reserved

Finding Fractions

Work with a classmate to take a fraction survey.
Look for six examples of fractions in your classroom
or school. Record your examples by describing each
finding below. Your partner rewrites the list of
findings as fractions. List the fractions in order
from the greatest to the least.

Example:

Finding: _____10 in line_____   Fraction: $\frac{3}{10}$ of those in line

_____3 girls_____   _____are girls._____

1. Finding: _____   Fraction: _____

    _____   _____

2. Finding: _____   Fraction: _____

    _____   _____

3. Finding: _____   Fraction: _____

    _____   _____

4. Finding: _____   Fraction: _____

    _____   _____

5. Finding: _____   Fraction: _____

    _____   _____

6. Finding: _____   Fraction: _____

    _____   _____

Addison-Wesley | All Rights Reserved

Name _____

Fractions on the Number Line

A mouse is crawling to the cheese.

1. Put the missing fractions on the number line.

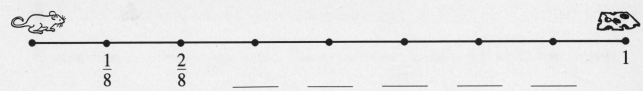

$\frac{1}{8}$ $\frac{2}{8}$ ____   ____   ____   ____   ____   1

2. Draw the mouse $\frac{1}{8}$ of the way to the cheese.

3. Draw it $\frac{1}{4}$ of the way.

4. Draw it $\frac{1}{2}$ of the way.

5. Draw it $\frac{7}{8}$ of the way.

Addison-Wesley | All Rights Reserved

Name _____

More and Less Pie

Dear Family,
   Your child has been learning about fractions. The exercises below give your child an opportunity to share with you the concept of comparing fractions. Practicing with fraction pieces at home will increase your child's progress in math.

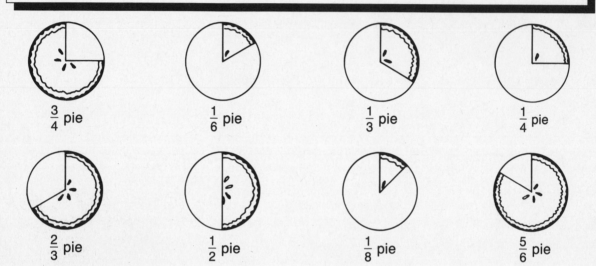

$\frac{3}{4}$ pie $\frac{1}{6}$ pie $\frac{1}{3}$ pie $\frac{1}{4}$ pie

$\frac{2}{3}$ pie $\frac{1}{2}$ pie $\frac{1}{8}$ pie $\frac{5}{6}$ pie

Write the fraction of pie each person had. Be sure to write **pie** in your answer.

1. Ron had more than $\frac{1}{6}$ pie but less than $\frac{1}{3}$ pie.

_____

2. David had less than $\frac{1}{2}$ pie but more than $\frac{1}{4}$ pie.

_____

3. Sean had more than $\frac{1}{2}$ pie but less than $\frac{3}{4}$ pie.

_____

4. Fran had more than $\frac{1}{3}$ pie but less than $\frac{2}{3}$ pie.

_____

5. Margaret had less than $\frac{5}{6}$ pie but more than $\frac{2}{3}$ pie.

_____

6. Cindy had less than $\frac{1}{4}$ pie but more than $\frac{1}{8}$ pie.

_____

Addison-Wesley | All Rights Reserved

Find the Fraction

1. What fraction of the dogs have

spots? _____

black ears? _____

spots and black ears? _____

2. What fraction of the shapes are

striped? _____

squares? _____

striped squares? _____

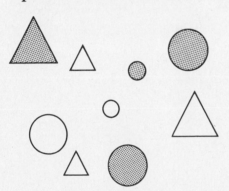

3. What fraction of the shapes are

shaded? _____

circles? _____

large? _____

shaded circles? _____

large circles? _____

shaded large circles? _____

4. What fraction of the children are wearing

skates? _____

striped shirts? _____

glasses? _____

skates and striped shirts? _____

skates and glasses? _____

Addison-Wesley | All Rights Reserved

Name _____

Coloring Eggs

To color $\frac{3}{4}$ of 12 eggs, follow these steps:

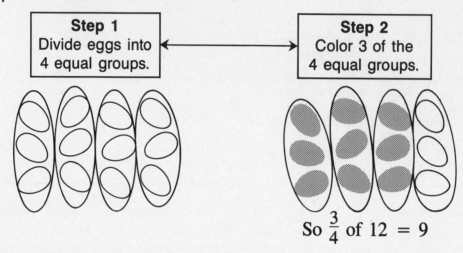

Step 1	Step 2
Divide eggs into 4 equal groups.	Color 3 of the 4 equal groups.

So $\frac{3}{4}$ of 12 = 9

Color each set below according to the fraction.
Remember to divide the eggs into equal groups first.
Then finish each equation.

1.

Color $\frac{3}{4}$ red.

$\frac{3}{4}$ of 8 = _____

2.

Color $\frac{2}{3}$ green.

$\frac{2}{3}$ of 6 = _____

3.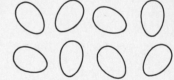

Color $\frac{2}{4}$ blue.

$\frac{2}{4}$ of 8 = _____

4.

Color $\frac{2}{5}$ yellow.

$\frac{2}{5}$ of 10 = _____

5.

Color $\frac{2}{3}$ red.

$\frac{2}{3}$ of 9 = _____

6.

Color $\frac{2}{4}$ green.

$\frac{2}{4}$ of 12 = _____

Addison-Wesley | All Rights Reserved

Pattern Pictures

Examine each group of numbers. What is the number pattern? Design a picture pattern to illustrate it.

Example:

Number Pattern: 4 8 12 16
Numbers increase by 4.

Picture:

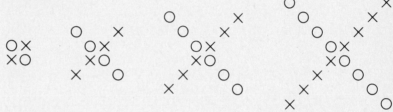

1. Number Pattern: 1 3 5 7 9

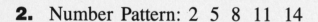   Picture:

2. Number Pattern: 2 5 8 11 14

_____   Picture:

3. Number Pattern: 2 6 10 14

_____   Picture:

Addison-Wesley | All Rights Reserved

Estimating Distance

In each exercise, a distance from A to B is shown. Follow the instructions to draw a line part of the way from one point to the other. Trace along the dotted line.

Draw a line to show:

1. a little less than $\frac{1}{2}$ the distance

A •·································· • B

2. a little more than $\frac{1}{2}$ the distance

A •·························• B

3. about $\frac{1}{4}$ the distance

A •···• B

4. about $\frac{2}{3}$ the distance

A •······································• B

5. about $\frac{3}{4}$ the distance

A •···• B

6. a little more than $\frac{1}{3}$ the distance

A •··• B

7. Look at the distance from A to B in Exercise 4. Use a straightedge to draw a line half as long.

8. How can you use a centimeter ruler to check that your answers are reasonable?

_____

_____

_____

Addison-Wesley | All Rights Reserved

How Does It Look?

Dear Family,
   We have just learned about mixed numbers (whole numbers and fractions). Help your child complete the drawings in these exercises. You may wish to think of other examples to draw with your child.

Draw a picture to illustrate the mixed number in each sentence.

1. Rita knit $1\frac{1}{3}$ mittens.	**2.** Len drank $2\frac{1}{5}$ glasses of water.
3. Clive painted $5\frac{3}{4}$ model cars.	**4.** Joy cut $4\frac{1}{4}$ butterflies out of paper.
5. Ling ate $9\frac{1}{2}$ strawberries.	**6.** Karen dyed $3\frac{2}{3}$ T-shirts.

Addison-Wesley | All Rights Reserved

Tic-Tac-Fractions

Play each tic-tac-fraction game. Add or subtract to complete each equation.
Identify the row with all the same answers. Draw a line across, down, or
diagonally through that row.

$\dfrac{3}{8} - \dfrac{2}{8} =$	$\dfrac{7}{8} - \dfrac{3}{8} =$	$\dfrac{5}{8} - \dfrac{2}{8} =$
$\dfrac{7}{8} - \dfrac{5}{8} =$	$\dfrac{1}{8} + \dfrac{1}{8} =$	$\dfrac{4}{8} - \dfrac{2}{8} =$
$\dfrac{1}{8} + \dfrac{4}{8} =$	$\dfrac{6}{8} + \dfrac{1}{8} =$	$\dfrac{2}{8} + \dfrac{4}{8} =$

$\dfrac{1}{7} + \dfrac{1}{7} =$	$\dfrac{2}{7} + \dfrac{2}{7} =$	$\dfrac{3}{7} - \dfrac{1}{7} =$
$\dfrac{5}{7} + \dfrac{1}{7} =$	$\dfrac{5}{7} - \dfrac{1}{7} =$	$\dfrac{4}{7} - \dfrac{1}{7} =$
$\dfrac{6}{7} - \dfrac{2}{7} =$	$\dfrac{1}{7} + \dfrac{3}{7} =$	$\dfrac{2}{7} + \dfrac{3}{7} =$

$\dfrac{1}{12} + \dfrac{3}{12} =$	$\dfrac{4}{12} + \dfrac{7}{12} =$	$\dfrac{2}{12} + \dfrac{5}{12} =$
$\dfrac{9}{12} - \dfrac{3}{12} =$	$\dfrac{7}{12} + \dfrac{1}{12} =$	$\dfrac{10}{12} - \dfrac{3}{12} =$
$\dfrac{8}{12} + \dfrac{3}{12} =$	$\dfrac{2}{12} - \dfrac{1}{12} =$	$\dfrac{1}{12} + \dfrac{6}{12} =$

Addison-Wesley | All Rights Reserved

Addison-Wesley | All Rights Reserved

Name _____

Decimal Driving

The car's gas tank is 0.4 full.
The gas gauge shows this.

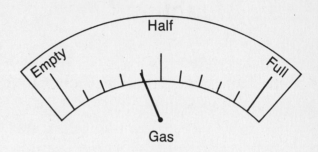

Show the hand on each gas gauge.

1.

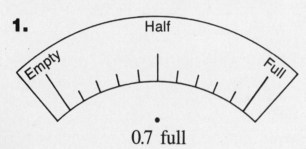

0.7 full

2.

0.2 full

3.

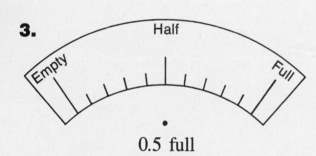

0.5 full

4.

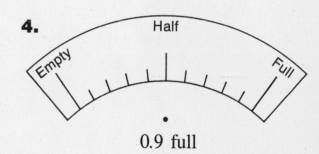

0.9 full

5.

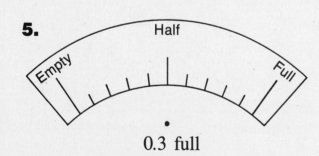

0.3 full

6.

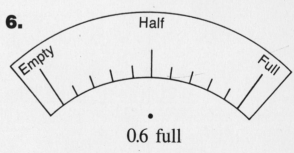

0.6 full

7. Sue and Charlie have driven 0.7 of the distance from the library to their house. Put an X on the map to show where their car is.

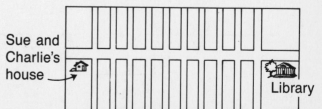

Using Tenths in Measurement

Joan had an odometer on her bicycle to measure how far she had gone. The dotted digit told her how many extra tenths of a kilometer she had traveled. Write the digits so that each odometer shows the correct reading.

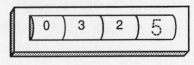

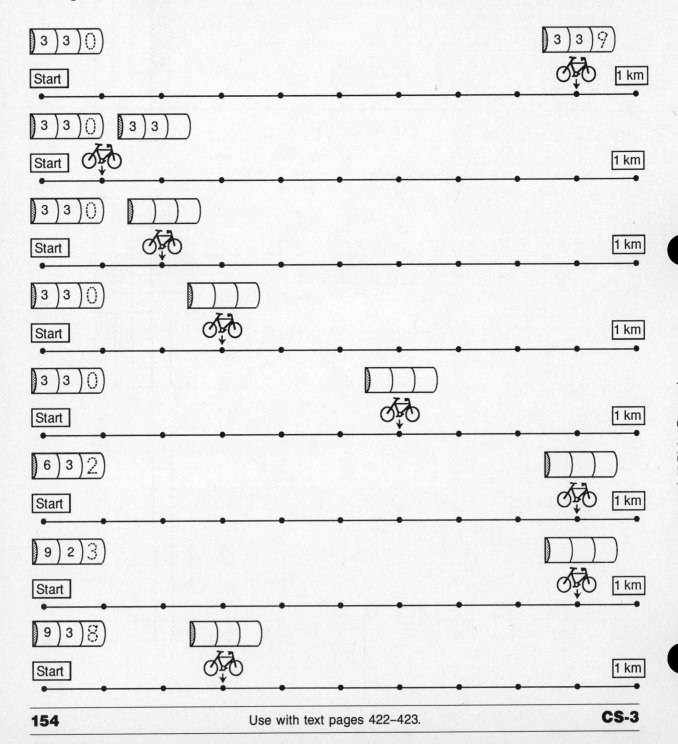

Addison-Wesley | All Rights Reserved

Decimal Designs

Create a picture for each grid
so that the shaded areas
represent the decimal.

Example: 0.17

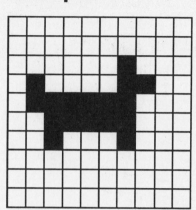

1. 0.30

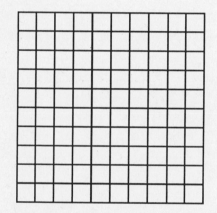

2. 0.45

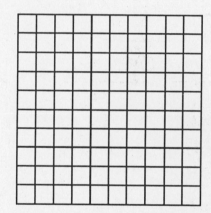

3. 0.15

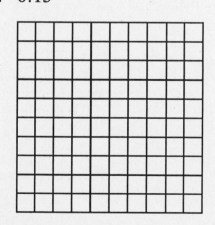

4. 0.72

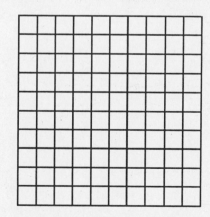

Addison-Wesley | All Rights Reserved

Name _____

Missing Decimals

Identify the missing decimal numbers. Write them in the boxes.

1. 3.2 +[ ] ⎯⎯ 10.7

2. 8.7 −[ ] ⎯⎯ 2.3

3. 7.1 +[ ] ⎯⎯ 13.0

4. 4.0 −[ ] ⎯⎯ 0.2

5. 6.2 +[ ] ⎯⎯ 16.0

6. [ ] − 4.5 ⎯⎯ 4.8

7. 1.5 +[ ] ⎯⎯ 4.2

8. [ ] − 3.7 ⎯⎯ 4.3

9. [ ] − 4.2 ⎯⎯ 1.6

10. 2.6 +[ ] ⎯⎯ 6.1

11. 9.4 −[ ] ⎯⎯ 2.7

12. [ ] + 8.5 ⎯⎯ 15.7

Now make up some exercises like these of your own. Have a classmate solve them and tell you how each was solved.

13. + ⎯⎯

14. + ⎯⎯

15. − ⎯⎯

16. − ⎯⎯

17. + ⎯⎯

18. − ⎯⎯

19. − ⎯⎯

20. + ⎯⎯

Addison-Wesley | All Rights Reserved

156   Use with text pages 426–427.   **CS-3**

Name _____

Hit the Slopes

Analyze each problem. Choose a strategy from the box. Complete the strategy sentence and solve the problem.

1. The ski boots are lined up in a row. Kirk's boots are in the middle. If Amy and Al's boots are to the right of his, how many pairs of boots are there in all?

I can _____.

Answer: _____

Some Strategies
Act It Out
Choose an Operation
Make an Organized List
Look for a Pattern
Use Logical Reasoning
Use Objects
Draw a Picture
Guess and Check
Make a Table
Work Backward

2. Ned can get a set of 3 lessons for $20. How much will it cost if Lisa and Paco each get a set of lessons, too?

I can _____.

Answer: _____

3. Tina skied 6 hours the first day. A storm on the second day brought her in after 2 hours. How many more hours did she ski on day one?

I can _____.

Answer: _____

4. A group of skiers came in to the lodge when it opened. Then 3 skiers left. When 4 more skiers arrived there were 10 in the lodge. How many skiers were in the lodge when it opened?

I can _____

_____.

Answer: _____

5. The skiers go down trails that are easy, average, or expert. They can go up the mountain on chair lifts, the gondola, or the T-bar. How many different choices do they have?

I can _____.

Answer: _____

Addison-Wesley | All Rights Reserved

Are They Compatible?

Decide whether the two numbers are compatible numbers
for division. Write **yes** or **no**.

1. 20 and 2 _____   **2.** 20 and 6 _____

3. 18 and 9 _____   **4.** 15 and 4 _____

5. 12 and 3 _____   **6.** 12 and 7 _____

7. 16 and 3 _____   **8.** 14 and 7 _____

9. 21 and 6 _____   **10.** 24 and 3 _____

11. 24 and 7 _____   **12.** 25 and 2 _____

13. 27 and 9 _____   **14.** 28 and 4 _____

15. 30 and 6 _____   **16.** 32 and 7 _____

17. 35 and 7 _____   **18.** 36 and 7 _____

19. 40 and 9 _____   **20.** 42 and 7 _____

21. Solve this problem using compatible numbers.

David and his 9 teammates scored 28 runs in a softball
game. They each scored about the same number of runs.

What compatible numbers could you use? _____

About how many did each teammate score? _____

22. Write your own definition of **compatible numbers**.

_____

_____

Addison-Wesley | All Rights Reserved

Name _____

Any Remainders?

Dear Family,
    Your child has been learning how to divide and find remainders.
Complete the following activity with your child to practice this skill.

Divide. Use small objects and cups to help you solve these.

1. $3\overline{)5}$ **2.** $2\overline{)7}$ **3.** $5\overline{)9}$ **4.** $3\overline{)8}$ **5.** $2\overline{)9}$

6. $4\overline{)19}$ **7.** $3\overline{)22}$ **8.** $4\overline{)30}$ **9.** $5\overline{)29}$ **10.** $2\overline{)17}$

11. $2\overline{)42}$ **12.** $3\overline{)69}$ **13.** $5\overline{)65}$ **14.** $4\overline{)72}$ **15.** $3\overline{)81}$

Solve.

16. How much does it cost for
1 speaker?

_____

17. How much does it cost for
1 tape?

_____

Answers: 1. 1 R2 2. 3 R1 3. 1 R4 4. 2 R2 5. 4 R1 6. 4 R3 7. 7 R1 8. 7 R2
9. 5 R4 10. 8 R1 11. 21 12. 23 13. 13 14. 18 15. 27 16. $23 17. $9

Addison-Wesley | All Rights Reserved

Is It Divisible?

1. Divide. Then ring the numbers that give a remainder of
0 when you divide by 2.

2)$\overline{10}$ 2)$\overline{11}$ 2)$\overline{12}$ 2)$\overline{13}$ 2)$\overline{14}$

2)$\overline{15}$ 2)$\overline{16}$ 2)$\overline{17}$ 2)$\overline{18}$ 2)$\overline{19}$

The numbers you ringed are divisible by _____ .

2. A number is divisible by 2 if it ends in _____ , _____ , _____ ,

_____ , or _____ .

3. Ring the numbers that are divisible by 2.

34   78   85   96   18   27   53   40

23   82   17   46   98   32   57   65

4. Divide. Then ring the numbers that give a remainder of 0
when you divide by 5.

5)$\overline{30}$ 5)$\overline{31}$ 5)$\overline{32}$ 5)$\overline{33}$

5)$\overline{35}$ 5)$\overline{36}$ 5)$\overline{37}$ 5)$\overline{38}$

5. A number is divisible by 5 if it ends in _____ or _____ .

6. Ring the numbers that are divisible by 5.

25   48   76   75   80   15   18   20

Addison-Wesley | All Rights Reserved

Climb the Mountain

Dear Family,
   Your child has been learning to check division problems by multiplication. Play the game below with your child to help sharpen this skill.

1. Copy and cut out the division squares.

2. Put them in a box or cup.

3. Each player puts a game marker on **Start**.

4. Take turns drawing a division square and dividing. Check the result by multiplying and adding the remainders.

5. Move the number of spaces in the remainder.

6. The first climber to reach the top colors the flag.

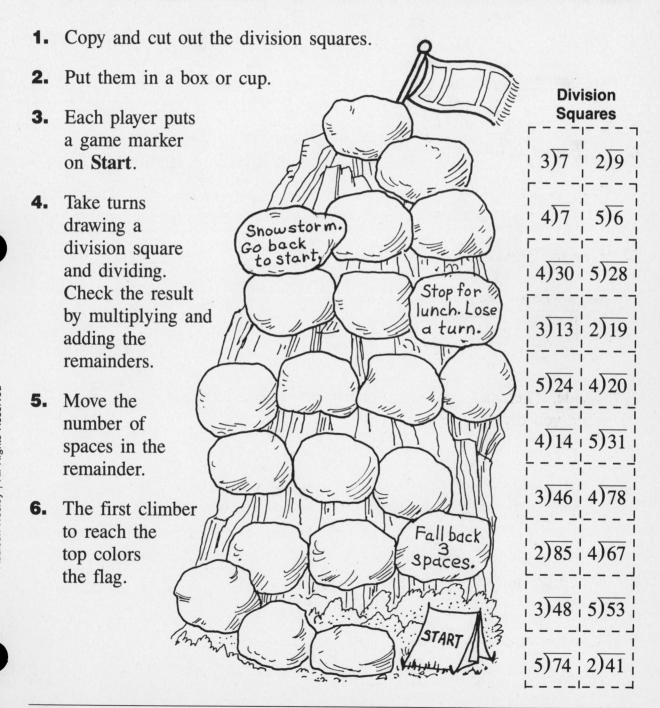

Division Squares

3)7̄	2)9̄
4)7̄	5)6̄
4)30̄	5)28̄
3)13̄	2)19̄
5)24̄	4)20̄
4)14̄	5)31̄
3)46̄	4)78̄
2)85̄	4)67̄
3)48̄	5)53̄
5)74̄	2)41̄

Addison-Wesley | All Rights Reserved

Writing Division Story Problems

Write a division story problem to match the data.
Then solve the problem.

Example: 23 slices of bread 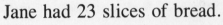 Jane had 23 slices of bread.
2 slices for each She used 2 slices to make each sandwich.
sandwich How many sandwiches could she make?

$$\begin{array}{r} 11\ \text{R1} \\ 2\overline{)23} \\ -2 \\ \hline 03 \\ -2 \\ \hline 1 \end{array}$$

Answer:
11 sandwiches

1. 19 slices of cheese
2 slices for each sandwich

_____

_____

_____

Answer: _____

2. 28 people
5 people fit in each car

_____

_____

_____

Answer: _____

3. 11 people
2 people for each umbrella

_____

_____

_____

Answer: _____

4. 35 crayons
4 crayons for each project

_____

_____

_____

Answer: _____

Addison-Wesley | All Rights Reserved

Build the Exercise

Fill in the ⬜s with the digits given to complete
each division exercise.

1. Use 1, 6, and 5.

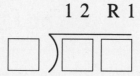

2. Use 7, 2, and 3.

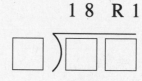

3. Use 7, 4, and 5.

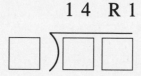

4. Use 5, 6, and 7.

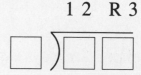

5. Use 9, 4, and 5.

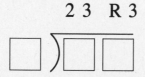

6. Use 3, 6, and 8.

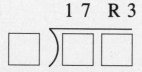

7. Use 8, 5, and 8.

8. Use 1, 4, 4, 5, and 8.

Addison-Wesley | All Rights Reserved

Name _____

Sale Signs

Finish the signs to match the estimates.

1.

Book Sale
☐ for $7.95

Joe estimated that
1 book costs about $2.

2.

Record Sale
☐ for $6.19

Sandra estimated that
1 record costs about $3.

3.

Game Sale
☐ for $4.89

Mindy estimated that
1 game costs about $1.

4.

Plant Sale
☐ for $14.95

Nan estimated that
1 plant costs about $5.

5.

Sweater Sale
☐ for $21.50

Steve estimated that
1 sweater costs about $7.

6.

Film Sale
☐ for $8.75

Rob estimated that
1 roll of film costs about $3.

7.

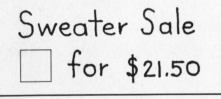

Tape Sale
☐ for $11.95

Rosa estimated that
1 tape costs about $6.

8.

Kite Sale
☐ for $12.25

Eric estimated that
1 kite costs about $4.

Addison-Wesley | All Rights Reserved

Use with text pages 450–451.